The Seven Principles of Man

&

Man and His Bodies

By
Annie Besant
edited by Dr. Jane Ma'ati Smith

ISBN # 1438258720 and EAN-13 # 9781438258720

The Seven Principles of Man

Contents

INTRODUCTION... 5

PRINCIPLE ONE-
THE DENSE PHYSICAL BODY... 7

PRINCIPLE TWO-
THE ETHERIC DOUBLE... 9

PRINCIPLE THREE-
PRÂNA, THE LIFE... 13

PRINCIPLE FOUR-
THE DESIRE BODY... 15

PRINCIPLE FIVE-
MANAS, THE THINKER, OR MIND... 20

PRINCIPLES SIX AND SEVEN-
ÂTMA – BUDDHI, THE SPIRIT... 45

INTRODUCTION

Man, according to the Theosophical teaching, is a sevenfold being, or, in the usual phrase, has a septenary constitution. Putting it in another way, man's nature has seven aspects, may be studied from seven different points of view, is composed of seven principles. The clearest and best way of all in which to think of man is to regard him as one, the Spirit or True Self; this belongs to the highest region of the universe, and is universal, the same for all; it is a ray of God, a spark from the divine fire. This is to become an individual, reflecting the divine perfection, a son that grows into the likeness of his father. For this purpose the Spirit, or true Self, is clothed in garment after garment, each garment belonging to a definite region of the universe, and enabling the Self to come into contact with that region, gain knowledge of it, and work in it. It thus gains experience, and all its latent potentialities are gradually drawn out into active powers. These garments, or sheaths, are distinguishable from each other both theoretically and practically. If a man be looked at clairvoyantly each is distinguishable by the eye, and they are separable each from each either during physical life or at death, according to the nature of any particular sheath. Whatever words may be used, the fact remains the same – that he is essentially sevenfold, an evolving being, part of whose nature has already been manifested, part remaining latent at present, so far as the vast majority of humankind is concerned. Man's consciousness is able to function through as many of these aspects as have been already evolved in him into activity.

This evolution, during the present cycle of human development, takes place on five out of seven planes of nature. The two higher planes – the sixth and seventh – will not be reached, save in the most exceptional cases, by men of this humanity in the present cycle, and they may therefore be left out of sight for our present purpose. As, however, some confusion has arisen as to the seven planes through differences of nomenclature, two diagrams are given at the end of this treatise showing the seven planes as they exist in our division of the universe, in correspondence with the vaster planes of the universe as a whole, and also the subdivision of the five into seven, as they are represented in some of our literature. A "plane" is merely a condition, a stage, a state; so that we might describe man as fitted by his nature, when that nature is fully developed, to exist consciously in seven different conditions, or seven different stages, in seven different states; or technically, on seven different planes of being. To take an easily verified illustration: a man may be conscious on the physical plane, that is, in his physical body, feeling hunger and thirst, and pain of a blow or cut. But let the man be a soldier in the heat of battle, and his consciousness will be centred in his passions and emotions, and he may suffer a wound without knowing it, his consciousness being away from the physical plane and acting on the plane of passions and emotions: when the excitement is over, consciousness will pass back to the physical, and he will "feel" the pain of his wound. Let the man be a philosopher, and as he ponders over some knotty problem he will lose all consciousness of bodily wants, of emotions, of love and hatred; his consciousness will have passed to the plane of intellect, he will be "abstracted", *i.e..,* drawn away from considerations pertaining to his bodily life, and fixed on the plane of thought. Thus may a man live on these several planes, in these several conditions, one part or another of his nature being thrown into activity at any given time; and an understanding of what man is, of his nature, his powers, his possibilities, will be reached more easily and assimilated more usefully if he is studied along these clearly defined lines, that if he be left without analysis, a mere confused bundle of qualities and states.

It has also been found convenient, having regard to man's mortal and immortal life, to put these seven principles into two groups – one containing the three higher principles and therefore called the Triad, the other containing the four lower, and therefore called the Quaternary. The Triad is the deathless part of man's nature, the "spirit" and soul of Christian terminology; the Quaternary is the mortal part, the "body", of Christianity. This division into body, soul and spirit is used by St. Paul, and is recognised in all careful Christian philosophy, although generally ignored by the mass of Christian people. In ordinary parlance soul and body make up the man, and the words soul and spirit are used interchangeably, with much confusion of thought as the result. This looseness is fatal to any clear view of the constitution of man, and the Theosophist may well appeal to the Christian philosopher as against the causal Christian non-thinker if it be urged that he is making distinctions difficult to be grasped. No philosophy worthy of the name can be stated even in the most elementary fashion without making some demand on the intelligence and the attention of the would be learner, and carefulness in the use of terms is a condition of all knowledge.

PRINCIPLE ONE
THE DENSE PHYSICAL BODY

The dense physical body of man is called the first of his seven principles, as it is certainly the most obvious. Built of material molecules, in the generally accepted sense of the term – with its five organs of sensation - the five senses - its organs of locomotion, its brain and nervous system, its apparatus for carrying on the various functions necessary for its continued existence, there is little to be said about this physical body in so slight a sketch as this of the constitution of man . Western science is almost ready to accept the Theosophical view that the human organism consists of innumerable "lives", which build up the cells. H.P.Blavatsky says on this: "Science has never yet gone so far as to assert with the Occult doctrine that our bodies, as well as those of animals, plants, and stones, are themselves altogether built up of such beings [bacteria, etc.]: which, with the exception of the larger species, no microscope can detect ….The physical and chemical constituents of all being found to be identical, chemical science may well say that there is no difference between the matter which composes the ox and that which forms the man. But the Occult doctrine is far more explicit. It says: Not only the chemical compounds are the same, but the same infinitesimal *invisible* lives compose the atoms of the bodies of the mountain and the daisy, of man and the ant, of the elephant and of the tree which shelters him from the sun. Each particle – whether you call it organic or inorganic – *is* a life. Every atom and molecule in the universe is both *life-giving and death-giving* to such forms. The microbes thus "build up the material body and its cells", under the constructive energy of vitality – a phrase that will be explained when we come to deal with "life", as the Third Principle, and with these microbes as part of it. When the "life" is no longer supplied the microbes "are left to run riot as destructive agents", and they break up and disintegrate the cells which they built, and so the body goes to pieces.

The purely physical consciousness is the consciousness of the cells and the molecules. The selective action of the cells, taking from the blood what they need, rejecting what they do not need, is an instance of this self consciousness. The process goes on without the help of our consciousness or volition. Again that which is called by physiologists unconscious memory is the memory of the physical consciousness, unconscious to us indeed, until we have learned to transfer our brain consciousness there. What we feel is not what the cells feel. The *pain* of a wound is felt by the brain-consciousness, acting, as before said, on the physical plane; but the consciousness of the molecule, as of the aggregation of molecules we call cells, leads it to hurry to the repair of the damaged tissues – actions of which the brain is *un*conscious – and its memory makes it repeat the same act again and again, even when it has become unnecessary. Hence cicatrices on wounds, scars, callosities, etc. The student may find many details on this subject in physiological treatises.

The death of the dense physical body occurs when the withdrawal of the controlling life-energy leaves the microbes to go their own way, and the many lives, no longer co-ordinated, separate from each other and scatter the particles of the cells of "the man of dust", and what we call decay sets in. The body becomes a whirlpool of unrestrained, unregulated lives, and its form, which resulted from their correlation, is destroyed by their exuberant individual energy. Death is but an aspect of life, and the destruction of one material form is but a prelude to building up of another.

For the ultimate in deeply transformative Chakra meditations
www.chakrahealingsounds.com

PRINCIPLE TWO
THE ETHERIC DOUBLE

The Linga Sharira , the astral body, the ethereal body, the fluidic body, the double, the wraith, the döppelganger, the astral man – such are a few of the many names which have been given to the second principle in man's constitution. The best name is the Etheric Double, because this term designates the second principle only, suggesting its constitution and appearance: whereas the other names have been used somewhat generally to describe bodies formed of some more subtle matter than that which affects our physical senses, without regard to the question whether other principles were or were not involved in their construction. I shall therefore use this name throughout.

The etheric double is formed of matter rarer or more subtle than that which is perceptible to our five senses, but still matter belonging to the physical plane, to which its functioning is confined. It is the state of physical matter, which is just beyond our "solid, liquid and gas", which form the dense portions of the physical plane.

This etheric double is the exact double or counterpart of the dense physical body to which it belongs, and is separable from it, although unable to go very far away there from. In normal healthy human beings the separation is a matter of difficulty, but in persons known as physical or materialising mediums, the ethereal double slips out without any great effort. When separated from the dense body it is visible to the clairvoyant as an exact replica thereof, united to it by a slender thread. So close is the physical union between the two that an injury inflicted on the etheric double appears as a lesion on the dense body, a fact known under the name of repercussion. A. d'Assier, in his well known work – translated by Colonel Olcott, the President-Founder of the Theosophical Society, under the title of *Posthumous Humanity* – gives a number of case in which this repercussion took place.

Separation of the etheric double from the dense body is generally accompanied by a considerable decrease in vitality in the latter, the double becoming more vitalised as the energy in the dense body diminishes. Colonel Olcott says:

" When the double is projected by a trained expert, even the body seems torpid, and the mind in a 'brown study' or dazed state; the eyes are lifeless in expression, the heart and lung actions feeble, and often the temperature much lowered. It is very dangerous to make any sudden noise or burst into the room, under such circumstances; for the double, being by instantaneous reaction drawn back into the body, the heart convulsively contracts, and death may even be caused."

In the case of Emilie Sagée the girl was noticed to look pale and exhausted when the double was visible: "the more distinct the double and more material in appearance, the really material person was effectively wearied, suffering and languid; when on the contrary, the appearance of the double weakened, the patient was seen to recover strength." This phenomenon is perfectly intelligible to the Theosophical student, who knows that the etheric double is the vehicle of the life-principle, or vitality, in the physical body, and that its partial withdrawal must therefore diminish the energy, with which this principle plays on the denser molecules. Clairvoyants, such as the Seeress of Prevorst, state that they can see the ethereal arm or leg attached to a body from which the dense limb has been amputated, and D'Assier remarks on this:

"Whilst I was absorbed in physiological studies, I was often arrested by a singular fact. It sometimes happens that a person who has lost an arm or leg experiences certain sensations at the extremities of the fingers and toes. Physiologists explain this anomaly by postulating in the patient an inversion of sensitiveness or of recollection, which makes him locate in the hand or the foot the sensation with which the nerve of the stump is alone affected …I confess that these explanations seemed to me laboured and have never satisfied me. When I studied the problem of the duplication of man, the question of amputations recurred to my mind, and I asked myself if it was not more simple and logical to attribute the anomaly of which I have spoken to the doubling of the human body, which by its fluid nature can escape amputation".

The etheric double plays a great part in spiritualistic phenomena. Here again the clairvoyant can help us. A clairvoyant can see the etheric double oozing out of the left side of the medium, and it is this which often appears as the "materialised spirit," easily moulded into various shapes by the thought-currents of the sitters, and gaining strength and vitality as the medium sinks into a deep trance. The Countess Wachtmeister, who is clairvoyant, says she has seen the same "spirit" recognised as that of a near relative or friend by different sitters, each of whom saw it according to his expectations, while to her own eyes it was the mere double of the medium. So again, H.P.Blavatsky told me that when she was at the Eddy homestead, watching the remarkable series of phenomena there produced, she deliberately moulded the "spirit" that appeared into the likenesses of persons known to herself and to no one else present, and the other sitters saw the types which she produced by her own will-power, moulding the plastic matter of the medium's etheric double.

Many of the movements of objects that occur at such séances, and at other times, without visible contact, are due to the action of the etheric double, and the student can learn how to produce such phenomena at will. They are trivial enough: the mere putting out of the etheric hand is no more important than the putting out of the dense counterpart, and neither more or less miraculous. Some persons produce such phenomena unconsciously, mere aimless overturnings of objects, making of noises, and so on: they have no control over their etheric double, and it just blunders about in their near neighbourhood, like a baby trying to walk. For the etheric double, like the dense body, has only a diffused consciousness belonging to its parts, and has no mentality. Nor does it readily serve as a medium of mentality, when disjoined from the dense counterpart.

This leads to and interesting point. The centres of sensation are located in the fourth principle, which may be said to form a bridge between the physical organs and the mental perceptions; impressions from the physical universe impinge on the material molecules of the dense physical body, setting in vibration the constituent cells of the organs of sensations, or our "senses". These vibrations, in their turn, set in motion the finer material molecules of the etheric double, in the corresponding sense organs of its finer matter. From these vibrations pass to the astral body, or fourth principle, presently to be considered, wherein are the corresponding centres of sensation. From these vibrations are again propagated into the yet rarer matter of the lower mental plane, whence they are reflected back until, reaching the material molecules of the cerebral hemispheres, they become our "brain consciousness". This correlated and unconscious succession is necessary for the normal action of consciousness as we know it. In sleep and in trance, natural or induced, the first two and the last stages are generally omitted, and the impressions start from and return to the astral plane, and thus make no trace on the brain memory; but the natural or trained psychic, the clairvoyant who does not need trance for the exercise of his powers, is able to transfer his consciousness from the physical to the astral plane without losing grip thereof, and can impress the brain-memory with knowledge gained on the astral plane, so retaining it for use.

Death means for the etheric double just what it means for the dense physical body, the breaking up of its constituent parts, the dissipation of its molecules. The vehicle of the vitality that animates the bodily organism as a whole, it oozes forth from the body when the death hour comes, and is seen by the clairvoyant as a violet light, or violet form, hovering over the dying person, still attached to the physical body by the slender thread before spoken of. When the thread snaps, the last breath has quivered outwards, and the bystanders whisper "He is dead".

The etheric double, being of physical matter, remains in the neighbourhood of the corpse, and is the "wraith", or "apparition", or "phantom", sometimes seen at the moment of death and afterwards by persons near the place where the death has occurred. It disintegrates slowly *pari passu* with its dense counterpart, and its remnants are seen by sensitives in cemeteries and church yards as violet lights hovering over graves. Here is one of the reasons which render cremation preferable to burial as a mode of disposing of the physical enveloped of man; the fire dissipates in a few hours the molecules which would otherwise be set free only in the slow course of gradual putrefaction, and thus quickly restores to their own plane the dense and etheric materials, ready for use once more in the building up of new forms.

PRINCIPLE THREE
PRÂNA, THE LIFE

All universes, all worlds, all men, all brutes, all vegetables, all minerals, all molecules and atoms, all that *is*, are plunged in a great ocean of life, life eternal, life infinite, life incapable of increase or diminution. The universe is only life in manifestation, life made objective, life differentiated. Now each organism, whether minute as a molecule or vast as a universe, may be thought of as appropriating to itself somewhat of life, of embodying, in itself as its own life some of this universal life . Figure a living sponge, stretching itself out in the water which bathes it, envelops it, permeates it; there is water, still the ocean, circulating in every passage, filling every pore; but we may think of the ocean outside the sponge, or of part of the ocean, appropriated by the sponge, distinguishing them in thought if we want to make statements about each severally. So each organism is a sponge bathed in the ocean of life universal, and containing within itself some of that ocean as its own breath of life. In Theosophy we distinguish this appropriated life under the name Prâna, breath, and call it the third principle in man's constitution.

To speak quite accurately, the "breath of life" – that which the Hebrews termed *Nephesh*, or the breath of life breathed into the nostrils of Adam – is not Prâna only, but Prâna and the fourth principle conjoined. It is these two together that make the "vital spark", and that are the "breath of life in man, as in beast or insect, or physical, material life". It is "the breath of animal life in man – the breath of life instinctual in the animal". But just now we are concerned with Prâna only, with vitality as the animating principle in all animal and human bodies. Of this life the etheric double is the vehicle, acting, so to say, as means of communication, as bridge, between Prâna and the dense body.

Prâna is explained in the *Secret Doctrine* as having for its lowest subdivision the microbes of science; these are the "invisible lives" that build up the physical cells; these are the "countless myriads of lives" that build the "tabernacle of clay", the physical bodies. "Science, dimly perceiving the truth, may find bacteria and other infinitesimals in the human body, and see in them only, occasional and abnormal visitors to which diseases are attributed. Occultism – which discerns a life in every atom and molecule, whether in a mineral or human body, in air, fire, or water – affirms that our whole body is built of such lives; the smallest bacterium under the microscope being to them a comparative size like an elephant to the tiniest infusoria". The "fiery lives" are the controllers and directors of these microbes, these invisible lives, and "indirectly" build, *i.e.,* build by controlling and directing the microbes, the immediate builders, supplying the latter with what is necessary, acting as the life of these lives; the "fiery lives" the synthesis, the essence, of Prâna, are the "vital constructive energy" that enables the microbes to build the physical cells. One of the archaic commentaries sums up the matter in stately and luminous phrases: "The worlds, to the profane, are built up of the known elements. To the conception of an Arhat, these elements are themselves collectively a divine life; distributively, on the plane of manifestations, the numberless and countless crores – (a crore is ten millions) – of lives. Fire alone is ONE, on the plane of the One Reality; on that of manifested, hence illusive, being, its particles are fiery lives which live and have their being at the expense of every other life that they consume. Therefore they are named the Devourers….Every visible thing in this universe was built by such lives, from conscious and divine primordial man, down to the unconscious agents that construct matter. From the One Life, formless and uncreate, proceeds the universe of lives. As in the universe, so in man, and all these countless lives, all this constructive vitality, all this is summed up by the Theosophist as Prâna .

Binaural Beat Chakra Meditation CD's and MP3's
www.chakrahealingsounds.com

PRINCIPLE FOUR
THE DESIRE BODY

In building up our man we have now reached the principle sometimes described as the animal soul, in Theosophical parlance Kâma Rûpa, or the desire-body. It belongs to in constitution, and functions on, the second or astral plane. It includes the whole body of appetites, passions, emotions, and desires which come under the head of instincts, sensations, feelings and emotions, in our Western psychological classification, and are dealt with as a subdivision of mind. In Western psychology mind is divided – by the modern school – into three main groups, feelings, will, intellect. Feelings are again divided into sensations and emotions, and these are divided and subdivided under numerous heads. Kâma, or desire, includes the whole group of "feelings", and might be described as our passional and emotional nature. All animal needs, such as hunger, thirst, sexual desire, come under it; all passions, such as love (in its lower sense), hatred, envy, jealousy. It is the desire for sentient experience, for experience of material joys – "the lust of the flesh, the lust of the eyes, the pride of life". This principle is the most material in our nature, it is the one that binds us fast to earthly life. "It is not molecularly constituted matter, least of all the human body, Sthula Sharîra, that is the grossest of all our 'principles' but verily the *middle* principle, the real animal centre; whereas our body is but its shell, the irresponsible factor and medium through which the beast in us acts all its life".

United to the lower part of Manas, the mind, as Kâma-Manas, it becomes the normal human brain-intelligence, and that aspect of it will be dealt with presently. Considered by itself, it remains the brute in us, the "ape and tiger" of Tennyson, the force which most avails to keep us bound to earth and to stifle in us all higher longings by the illusions of sense.

Kâma joined to Prâna is, as we have seen, the "breath of life," the vital sentient principle spread over every particle of the body. It is, therefore, the seat of sensation, that which enables the organs of sensation to function. We have already noted that the physical organs of sense, the bodily instruments that come into immediate contact with the external world, are related to the organs of sensation in the etheric double. But these organs would be incapable of functioning did not Prâna make them vibrant with activity, and their vibrations would remain vibrations only, motion on the material plane of the physical body, did not Kâma, the principle of sensation translate the vibration into feeling. Feeling indeed, is consciousness on the kâmic plane, and when a man is under the dominion of a sensation or a passion, the Theosophist speaks of him as on the kâmic plane, meaning thereby that his consciousness is functioning on that plane. For instance, a tree may reflect rays of light, that is, ethereal vibrations, and these vibrations striking on the outer eye will set up vibrations in the physical nerve-cells; these will be propagated as vibrations to the physical and on to the astral centres, but there is no *sight* of the tree until the seat of the sensation is reached, and Kâma enables us to *perceive*.

Matter of the astral plane – including that called elemental essence – is the material of which the desire-body is composed, and it is the peculiar properties of this matter which enable it to serve as the sheath in which the Self can gain experience of sensation. (The constitution of the elemental essence, would lead us too far from an elementary treatise). The desire–body, or astral body, as it is often called, has the form of a mere cloudy mass during the earlier stages of evolution, and is incapable of serving as an independent vehicle of consciousness. During deep sleep it escapes from the physical body, but remains near it, and the mind within it is almost as much asleep as the body. It is, however, liable to be affected by forces of the astral plane akin to its own constitution, and gives rise to dreams of a sensuous kind.In a man of average intellectual development the desire-body has become more highly organised, and when separated from the physical body is seen to resemble it is outline and features; even then, however, it is not conscious of its surroundings on the astral plane, but encloses the mind as a shell, within which the mind may actively function, while not yet able to use it as an independent vehicle of consciousness. Only in the highly evolved man does the desire-body become thoroughly organised and vitalised, as much the vehicle of consciousness on the astral plane as the physical body is on the physical plane.

After death, the higher part of man dwells for awhile in the desire-body, the length of its stay depending on the comparative grossness or delicacy of its constituents. When the man escapes from it, it persists for a time as a "shell" and when the departed entity is of a low type, and during earth life infused such mentality as it possessed into the passional nature, some of this remains entangled with the shell. It then possesses consciousness of a very low order, has brute cunning, is without conscience – an altogether objectionable entity, often spoken of as a "spook." It strays about, attracted to all places in which animal desires are encouraged and satisfied, and is drawn into the currents of those whose animal passions are strong and unbridled. Mediums of low type inevitably attract these eminently undesirable visitors, whose fading vitality is reinforced in their séance rooms, who catch astral reflections, and play the part of "disembodied spirits" of a low order. Nor is this all; if at such a séance there be present some man or woman of correspondingly low development, the spook will be attracted to that person, and may attach itself to him or to her, and thus may be set up currents between the desire-body of the living person and the dying desire-body of the dead person, generating results of the most deplorable kind.

The longer or shorter persistence of the desire-body as a shell or a spook depends on the greater or less development of the animal and passional nature in the dying personality. If during earth-life the animal nature was indulged and allowed to run riot, if the intellectual and spiritual parts of man were neglected or stifled, then, as the life-currents were set strongly in the direction of passion, the desire-body will persist for a long period after the body of the person is dead. Or again, if earth-life has been suddenly cut short by accident or by suicide, the link between Kâma and Prâna will not be easily broken, and the desire-body will be strongly vivified. If, on the other hand, desire has been conquered and bridled during earth-life, if it has been purified and trained into subservience to man's higher nature, then there is but little to energise the desire-body and it will quickly disintegrate and dissolve away.

There remains one other fate, terrible in its possibilities, which may befall the fourth principle, but it cannot be clearly understood until the fifth principle has been dealt with.

THE QUATERNARY, OR FOUR LOWER PRINCIPLES

[The etheric double is here named the Linga Sharira, a name now discarded in consequence of the confusion caused by employing a well-known term in Hindu philosophy in an entirely new sense. Before her departure H.P.B. urged her pupils to reform the terminology, which had been too carelessly put together, and we are trying to carry out her wish.]

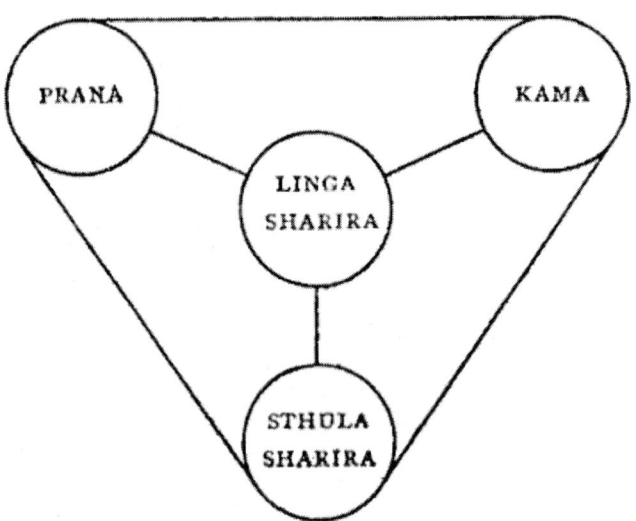

We have thus studied man, as to his lower nature, and have reached the point in his path of evolution to which he is accompanied by the brute. The quaternary, regarded alone, ere it is affected by contact with the mind, is merely a lower animal; it awaits the coming of the mind to make it man. Theosophy teaches that through past ages man was thus slowly built up, stage by stage, principle by principle, until he stood as a quaternary, brooded over but not in contact with the Spirit, waiting for that mind which could alone enable him to progress farther, and to come into conscious union with the Spirit, so fulfilling the very object of his being. This aeonian evolution, in its slow progression, is hurried through in the personal evolution of each human being, each principle which was in the course of ages successively evolved in man on earth, appearing as part of the constitution of each man at the point of evolution reached at any given time, the remaining principles being latent, awaiting their gradual manifestation. The evolution of the quaternary until it reached the point at which further progress was impossible without mind, is told in eloquent sentences in the archaic stanzas on which the *Secret Doctrine* of H.P. Blavatsky is based (*breath* is, the Spirit, for which the human tabernacle is to be built; the *gross body* is the dense physical body; the *spirit of life* is Prâna; the *mirror of its body* is the etheric double; the *vehicle of desires is* Kâma):

"The Breath needed a form; the Fathers gave it. The Breath needed a gross body; the Earth moulded it; The Breath needed the Spirit of Life; the Solar Lhas breathed into it its form. The Breath needed a Mirror of its Body; 'We gave it our own', said the Dhyânis. The Breath needed a Vehicle of Desires; 'It has it', said the Drainer of Waters. But Breath needs a Mind to embrace the Universe; 'We cannot give that,'said the fathers, 'I never had it ,' said the Spirit of the Earth. 'The form would be consumed were I to give it mine,' said the Great Fire. .Man remained an empty senseless Bhûta" (phantom).

And so is the personal man without mind. The quaternary alone is not man, the Thinker, and it is as Thinker that man is really man.

Yet at this point let the student pause, and reflect over the human constitution, so far as he has gone. For this quaternary is the mortal part of man, and is distinguished by Theosophy as the *personality*. It needs to be very clearly and definitely realised, if the constitution of man is to be understood, and if the student is to read more advanced treatises with intelligence. True, to make the personality *human* it has yet to come under the rays of mind, and to be illuminated by it as the world by the rays of the sun. But even without these rays it is a clearly defined entity, with its dense body, its etheric double, its life, and its desire body or animal soul. It has passions, but no reason; it has emotions, but no intellect; it has desires, but no rationalised will; it awaits the coming of its monarch, the mind, the touch which shall transform it into man.

PRINCIPLE FIVE
MANAS, THE THINKER, OR MIND

We have reached the most complicated part of our study, and some thought and attention are necessary from the reader to gain even an elementary idea of the relation held by the fifth principle to the other principles in man.

The word Manas comes from the Sanskrit word *man,* the root of the verb to think; it is the Thinker in us, spoken of vaguely in the West as mind. I will ask the reader to regard Manas as Thinker rather than as mind, because the word Thinker suggests some one who thinks, *i.e.,* an individual, an entity. And this is exactly the Theosophical idea of Manas, for Manas is the immortal individual, the real " I", that clothes itself over and over again in transient personalities, and itself endures for ever. It is described in the *Voice of the Silence* in the exhortation addressed to the candidate for initiation: "Have perseverance as one who doth for evermore endure. Thy shadows [personalities] live and vanish; that which in thee shall live for ever, that which in thee *knows*, for it is knowledge, is not of fleeting life; it is the man that was, that is, and will be, for whom the hour shall never strike". H.P.Blavatsky has described it very clearly in the *Key to Theosophy*: "Try to imagine a 'Spirit', a celestial being, whether we call it by one name or another, divine in its essential nature, yet not pure enough to be one with the ALL, and having, in order to achieve this, to so purify its nature as finally to gain that goal. It can do so only be passing *individually* and *personally*, *i.e.*, spiritually and physically, through every experience and feeling that exists in the manifold or differentiated universe. It has, therefore, after having gained such experience in the lower kingdoms, and having ascended higher and still higher with every rung on the ladder of being, to pass through every experience on the human planes. In its very essence it is Thought, and is, therefore, called in its plurality *Manasaputra*, 'the Sons of (universal) Mind.' This *individualised* 'Thought' is what we Theosophists call the *real* human Ego, the thinking entity imprisoned in a case of flesh and bones. This is surely a spiritual entity, not *matter* [that is, not matter as we know it, on the plane of the objective universe] – and such entities are the incarnating Egos that inform the bundle of animal matter called mankind, and whose names are *Manasa* or minds".

This idea may be rendered yet clearer perhaps by a hurried glance cast backward over man's evolution in the past. When the quaternary had been slowly built up, it was a fair house without a tenant, and stood empty awaiting the coming of the one who was to dwell therein.The name Mânasaputra (the sons of mind) covers many grades of intelligence, ranging from the mighty "Sons of the Flame" whose human evolution lies far behind them, down to those entities who gained individualisation in the cycle preceding our own, and were ready to incarnate on this earth in order to accomplish their human stage of evolution. Some superhuman intelligences incarnated as guides and teachers of our infant humanity, and became founders and divine rulers of the ancient civilisations. Large numbers of the entities spoken of above, who had already evolved some mental faculties, took up their abode in the human quaternary, in the mindless men. These are the reincarnating Mânasaputra, who became the tenants of the human frames as then evolved on earth, and these same Mânasaputra, reincarnating age after age, are the Reincarnating Egos, the Manas in us, the persistent individual, the fifth principle in man.The remainder of mankind through successive ages received from the loftier Mânasaputra their first spark of mind, a ray which stimulated into growth the germ of mind latent within them, the human soul thus having its birth in time there. It is these differences of age, as we may call them, in the beginning of the individual life, of the specialisation of the eternal Divine Spirit into a human soul, which explain the enormous differences in mental capacity found in our present humanity.

The multiplicity of names given to this fifth principle has probably tended to increase the confusion surrounding it in the minds of many who are beginning to study Theosophy. *Mânasaputra* is what we call the historical name, the name that suggests the entrance into humanity of a class of already individualised souls at a certain point of evolution; *Manas* is the ordinary name, descriptive of the intellectual nature of the principle; the *Individual* or the " I ", or *Ego*, recalls the fact that this principle is permanent, does not die, is the individualising principle, separating itself in thought from all that is not itself, the *Subject* in Western terminology as opposed to the *Object*; the *Higher Ego* puts it into contrast with the *Personal Ego*, of which something is to be presently said .The *Reincarnating Ego* lays stress on the fact that it is the principle that reincarnates continually, and so unites in its own experience all the lives passed through on earth. There are various other names, but they will not be met with in elementary treatises. The above are those most often encountered, and there is no real difficulty about them, but when they are used interchangeably, without explanation, the unhappy student is apt to tear his hair in anguish, wondering how many principles he has got hold of, and what relation they bear to each other.

We must now consider Manas during a single incarnation, which will serve as the type of all, and we will start when the Ego has been drawn – by causes set a-going in previous earth-lives – to the family in which is to be born the human being who is to serve as its next tabernacle. (I do not deal here with reincarnation, since that great and most essential doctrine of Theosophy must be expounded separately). The Thinker, then, awaits the building of the "house of life" which he is to occupy; and now arises a difficulty; himself a spiritual entity living on the mental or third plane upwards, a plane far higher than that of the physical universe, he cannot influence the molecules of gross matter of which his dwelling is built by the direct play upon them of his own most subtle particles. So, he projects part of his own substance, which clothes itself with astral matter, and then with the help of etheric matter permeates the whole nervous system of the yet unborn child, to form, as the physical apparatus matures, the thinking principle in man. This projection from Manas, spoken of as its reflection, its shadow, its ray, and by many another descriptive and allegorical name, is the lower Manas, in contradistinction to the higher Manas – Manas, during every period of incarnation, being dual. On this, H.P.Blavatsky says: "Once imprisoned, or incarnate, their (the Manas) essence becomes dual; that is to say the *rays* of the eternal divine Mind, considered as individual entities, assume a twofold attribute which is (a) their essential, inherent, characteristic, heaven-aspiring mind (higher Manas), and (b) the human quality of thinking, or animal cogitation, rationalised owing to the superiority of the human brain, the Kâma-tending or lower Manas".

We must now turn our attention to this lower Manas alone, and see the part which it plays in the human constitution.

It is engulfed in the quaternary, and we may regard it as clasping Kâma with one hand, while with the other it retains its hold on its father, the higher Manas. Whether it will be dragged down by Kâma altogether and be torn away from the triad to which by its nature it belongs, or whether it will triumphantly carry back to its source the purified experiences of its earth-life – that is the life-problem set and solved in each successive incarnation. During earth-life, Kâma and the lower Manas are joined together, and are often spoken of conveniently as Kâma-Manas. Kâma supplies, as we have seen, the animal and passional elements; the lower Manas rationalises these, and adds the intellectual faculties; and so we have the brain-mind, the brain-intelligence, *i.e.,* Kâma-Manas functioning in the brain and nervous system, using the physical apparatus as its organ on the material plane.In man these two principles are interwoven during life, and rarely act separately, but the student must realise that "Kâma-Manas" is not a new principle, but the interweaving of the fourth with the lower part of the fifth.

As with a flame we may light a wick, and the colour of the flame of the burning wick will depend on the nature of the wick and of the liquid in which it is soaked, so in each human being the flame of Manas set alight the brain and Kâmic wick, and the colour of the light from that wick will depend on the Kâmic nature and the development of the brain-apparatus.If the Kâmic nature be strong and undisciplined it will soil the pure manasic light, lending it a lurid tinge and fouling it with noisome smoke. If the brain-apparatus be imperfect or undeveloped, it will dull the light and prevent it from shining forth to the outer world. As was clearly stated by H.P.Blavatsky in her article on "Genius"; "What we call 'the manifestations of genius' in a person are only the more or less successful efforts of that Ego to assert itself on the outward plane of its objective form – the man of clay – in the matter-of-fact daily life of the latter. The Egos of a Newton, an Aeschylus, or a Shakespeare

are of the same essence and substance as the Egos of a yokel, an ignoramus, a fool, or even an idiot; and the self-assertion of their informing *genii* depends on the physiological and material construction of the physical man. No Ego differs from another Ego in its primordial or original essence and nature. That which makes of one mortal a great man and of another a vulgar silly person is, as said, the quality and make-up of the physical shell or casing, and the adequacy or inadequacy of brain and body to transmit and give expression to the light of the real *inner* man; and this aptness or inaptness is, in its turn, the result of Karma. Or, to use another simile, physical man is the musical instrument, and the Ego the performing artist. The potentiality of perfect melody of sound is in the former – the instrument – and no skill of the latter can awaken a faultless harmony out of a broken or badly made instrument. This harmony depends on the fidelity of transmission, by word and act, to the objective plane, of the unspoken divine thought in the very depths of man's subjective or inner nature. Physical man may – to follow our simile – be a priceless Stradivarius, or a cheap and cracked fiddle, or again a mediocrity between the two, in the hands of the Paganini who ensouls him".

Bearing in mind these limitations and idiosyncrasies [Limitations and idiosyncrasies due to the action of the Ego in previous earth-lives, be it remembered] imposed on the manifestations of the thinking principle by the organ through which it has to function, we shall have little difficulty in following the workings of the lower Manas in man; mental ability, intellectual strength, acuteness, subtlety – all these are its manifestations; these may reach as far as what is often called genius, what H.P. Blavatsky speaks of as "artificial genius, the outcome of culture and of purely intellectual acuteness". Its nature is often demonstrated by the presence of Kâmic elements in it, of passion, vanity and arrogance.

The higher Manas can but rarely manifest itself at the present stage of human evolution. Occasionally a flash from those loftier regions lightens the twilight in which we dwell, and such flashes alone are what the Theosophist calls true genius; "Behold in every manifestation of genius, *when combined with virtue*, the undeniable presence of the celestial exile, the divine Ego whose jailer thou art,

O man of matter." For theosophy teaches "that the presence in man of various creative powers" – called genius in their collectivity – is due to no blind chance, to no innate qualities through hereditary tendencies – though that which is known as atavism may often intensify these faculties – but to an accumulation of individual antecedent experiences of the Ego in its preceding life and lives. For, omniscient in its essence and nature, it still requires experience, through its *personalities*, of the things of earth, earthly on the objective plane, in order to apply the fruition of that abstract experience to them. And, adds our philosophy, the cultivation of certain aptitudes through out a long series of past incarnations must finally culminate, in some one life, in a blooming forth as *genius,* in one or another direction". For the manifestation of true genius, purity of life is an essential condition.

Kâma-Manas is the personal self of man; we have already seen that the quaternary, as a whole, is the personality, "the shadow". and the lower Manas gives the individualising touch that makes the personality recognise itself as "I". It becomes intellectual, it recognises itself as separate from all other selves; deluded by the separateness it *feels*, it does not realise a unity beyond all that it is able to sense. And the lower Manas, attracted by the vividness of the material-life impressions, swayed by the rush of the Kâmic emotions, passions and desires, attracted to all material things blinded and deafened by the storm voices among which it is plunged – the lower Manas is apt to forget the pure and serene glory of its birthplace, and to throw itself into the turbulence which gives rapture in lieu of peace. And, be it remembered, it is this very lower Manas that yields the last touch of delight to the senses and to the animal nature; for what is passion that can neither anticipate nor remember, where is ecstasy without the subtle force of imagination, the delicate colours of fancy and of dream?

But there may be chains yet more strong and constraining, binding the lower Manas fast to the earth. They are forged of ambition, of desire for fame, be it for that of the statesman's power, or of supreme intellectual achievement. So long as any work is wrought for sake of love, or praise, or even recognition that the work is "mine" and not another's; so long as in the heart's remotest chambers one subtlest yearning remains to be recognised as separate from all; so long, however grand the ambition, however far reaching the charity, however lofty the achievement, Manas is tainted with Kâma, and is not pure as its source.

MANAS IN ACTIVITY

We have already seen that the fifth principle is dual in its aspect during each period of earth-life, and that the lower Manas united to Kâma, spoken of conveniently as Kâma-Manas, functions in the brain and nervous system of man. We need to carry our investigation a little further in order to distinguish clearly between the activity of the higher and of the lower Manas, so that the working in the mind of man may become less obscure to us that it is at present to many.

Now the cells of the brain and nervous system (like all other cells) are composed of minute particles of matter, called molecules (literally, little heaps). These molecules do not touch each other, but are held grouped together by that manifestation of the Eternal Life which we call attraction. Not being in contact with each other they are able to vibrate to and fro if set in motion, and, as a matter of fact, they are in a state of continual vibration. H.P.Blavatsky points out that molecular motion is the lowest and most material form of the One Eternal Life. Itself motion as the "Great Breath", and the source of all motion on every plane of the universe. In the Sanskrit, the roots of the terms for spirit, breath, being and motion are essentially the same, and Râma Prâsad says that "all these roots have for their origin the sound produced by the breath of animals" – the sound of expiration and inspiration.

Now, the lower mind, or Kâma-Manas, acts on the molecules of the nervous cells by motion, and set them vibrating, so starting mind-consciousness on the physical plane. Manas itself could not affect these molecules ; but its ray, the lower Manas, having clothed itself in astral matter and united itself to the kâmic elements, is able to set the physical molecules in motion, and so give rise to "brain consciousness," including the brain memory and all other functions of the human mind, as we know it in its ordinary activity. These manifestations, "like all other phenomena on the material plane *must* be related in their final analysis to the world of vibration," says H.P.Blavatsky. But, she goes on to point out , "in their origin they belong to a different and higher world of harmony". Their origin is in the manasic essence, in the ray; but on the material plane, acting on the molecules of the brain, they are translated into vibrations.

This action of the Kâma-Manas is spoken of by Theosophists as *psychic*. All mental and passional activities are due to this psychic energy, and its manifestations are necessarily conditioned by the physical apparatus through which it acts. We have already seen this broadly stated, and the *rationale* of the statement will now be apparent. If the molecular constitution of the brain be fine, and if the working of the specifically kâmic organs (liver, spleen, etc.) be healthy and pure – so as not to injure the molecular constitution of the nerves which put them into communication with the brain – then the psychic breath, as it sweeps through the instrument, awakens in this true Aeolian harp harmonious and exquisite melodies; whereas if the molecular constitution be gross or poor, if it be disordered by the emanations of alcohol, if the blood be poisoned by gross living or sexual excesses, the strings of the Aeolian harp become too loose or too tense, clogged with dirt or frayed with harsh usage, and when the psychic breath passes over them they remain dumb or give out harsh discordant notes, not because the breath is absent, but because the strings are in evil case.

It will now, I think, be clearly understood that what we call mind, or intellect, is in H.P.Blavatsky's words, "a pale and too often distorted reflection" of Manas itself, or our fifth principle; Kâma-Manas is "the rational, but earthly or physical intellect of man, incased in, and bound by, matter, therefore subject to the influence of the latter"; it is the "lower self, or that which manifesting through our *organic* system, acting on this plane of illusion, imagines itself the *Ego sum*, and thus falls into what Buddhist philosophy brands as the 'heresy of separateness.' It is the human personality, from which proceeds "the psychic, *i.e.,* 'terrestrial wisdom' at best, as it is influenced by all the chaotic stimuli of the human or rather animal passions of the living body".

A clear understanding of the fact that Kâma-Manas belongs to the human personality, that it functions in and through the physical brain, that it acts on the molecules of the brain, setting them into vibration, will very much facilitate the comprehension by the student of the doctrine of reincarnation. That great subject will be dealt with in another volume of this series, and I do not propose to dwell upon it here, more than to remind the student to take careful note of the fact that the lower Manas is a ray from the immortal Thinker, *illuminating a personality*, and that all the functions which are brought into activity in the brain-consciousness are functions correlated to the particular brain, to the particular personality, in which they occur.The brain-molecules that are set vibrating are material organs in the man of flesh; they did not exist as brain molecules before his conception, nor do they persist as brain molecules after his disintegration. Their functional activity is limited by the limits of his personal life, the life of the body, the life of the transient personality.

Now the faulty of which we speak as memory on the physical plane depends on the response of these very brain-molecules to the impulse of the lower Manas, and there is no link between the brains of successive personalities except through the higher Manas, that sends out its ray to inform and enlighten them successively. It follows, then, inevitably, that unless the consciousness of man can rise from the physical and Kâma-manasic planes to the plane of the higher Manas, no memory of one personality can reach over to another. The memory of the personality belongs to the transitory part of man's complex nature, and those only can recover the memory of their past lives who can raise their consciousness to the plane of the immortal Thinker, and can, so to speak, travel in consciousness up and down the ray which is the bridge between the personal man that perishes and the immortal man that endures. If, while we are cased in the human flesh, we can raise our consciousness along the ray that connects our lower with our true Self, and so reach the higher Manas, we find there stored in the memory of that eternal Ego the whole of our past lives on earth, and we can bring back those records to our brain-memory by way of that same ray, through which we can climb upwards to our "Father".

But this is an achievement that belongs to a late stage of human evolution, and until this is reached the successive personalities informed by the manasic rays are separated from each other, and no memory bridges over the gulf between. The fact is obvious enough to any one who thinks the matter out, but as the difference between the personality and the immortal individuality is somewhat unfamiliar in the West, it may be well to remove a possible stumbling-block from the student's path.

Now the lower Manas may do one of three things; It may rise towards its source, and by unremitting and strenuous efforts become one with its "Father in heaven," or the higher Manas – Manas uncontaminated with earthly elements, unsoiled and pure. Or it may partially aspire and partially tend downwards, as indeed is mostly the case with the average man. Or saddest fate of all, it may become so clogged with the kâmic elements as to become one with them, and be finally wrenched away from its parent and perish.

Before considering these three fates, there are a few more words to be said touching the activity of the lower Manas.

As the lower Manas frees itself from Kâma, it becomes the sovereign of the lower part of man, and manifests more and more of its true and essential nature. In Kâma is desire, moved by bodily needs, and Will, which is the outgoing energy of the Self in Manas, is often led captive by the turbulent physical impulses. But the lower Manas, "whenever it disconnects itself, for the time being, from Kâma, becomes the guide of the highest mental faculties, and is the organ of the free will in physical man". But the condition of this freedom is that Kâma shall be subdued, shall lie prostrate beneath the feet of the conqueror; if the maiden Will is to be set free, the manasic St. George must slay the kâmic dragon that holds her captive; for while Kâma is unconquered, Desire will be master of the Will.

Again, as the lower Manas frees itself from Kâma, it becomes more and more capable of transmitting to the human personality with which it is connected the impulses that reach it from its source. It is then, as we have seen, that genius flashes forth, the light from the higher Ego streaming through the lower Manas to the brain, and manifesting itself to the world. So also, as H.P.Blavatsky points out, such action may raise a man above the normal level of human power. "The higher Ego", she says, "cannot act directly on the body, as its consciousness belongs to quite another plane and planes of ideation; the lower self does; and its action and behaviour depend on its freewill and choice as to whether it will gravitate more towards its parent ('the Father in heaven') or the 'animal' which it informs, the man of flesh. The higher Ego, as part of the essence of the Universal Mind, is unconditionally omniscient on its own plane, and only potentially so in our terrestrial sphere, as it has to act solely through its *alter ego* the personal self. Now …the former is the vehicle of all knowledge of the past, the present and the future, and it is from this fountain head that its 'double' catches occasional glimpses of that which is beyond the senses of man, and transmits them to certain brain-cells (unknown to science in their functions), thus making of man a *seer*, a soothsayer and a prophet". This is the real seership, and on it a few words must be said presently. It is, naturally, extremely rare, and precious as it is rare. A "faint and distorted reflection" of it is found in what is called mediumship, and of this H.P.Blavatsky says: "Now what is a medium? The term medium, when not applied to things and objects, is supposed to be a person through whom the action of another person or being is either manifested or transmitted. Spiritualists believing in communications with disembodied spirits, and that these can manifest through, or impress sensitives to transmit messages from them, regard mediumship as a blessing and a great privilege. We Theosophists, on the other hand, who do not believe in the 'communion of spirits', as Spiritualists do, regard the gift as one of the most dangerous of abnormal nervous diseases. A medium is simply one in whose personal Ego, or terrestrial mind, the percentage of the astral light so preponderates as to impregnate with it his whole physical constitution. Every organ and cell thereby is attuned, so to speak, and subject to an enormous and abnormal tension".

To return to the three fates spoken of above, any one of which may befall the lower Manas.

It may rise towards its source and become one with the Father in heaven. This triumph can only be gained by many successive incarnations, all consciously directed towards this end. As life succeeds life, the physical frame becomes more and more delicately attuned to vibrations responsive to the manasic impulses, so that gradually the manasic ray needs less and less of the coarser astral matter as its vehicle."It is part of the mission of the manasic ray to get gradually rid of the blind deceptive element which, though it makes of it an actual spiritual entity on this plane, still brings it into so close contact with matter as to entirely becloud its divine nature and stultify its intuitions". Life after life it rids itself of this "blind deceptive element", until at least, master of Kâma, and with body responsive to mind, the ray becomes one with its radiant source, the lower nature is wholly attuned to the higher, and the Adept stands forth complete, the "Father and the Son", having become one on all planes, as they have been always "one in heaven". For him the wheel of incarnation is over, the cycle of necessity is trodden. Henceforth he can incarnate at will, to do any special service to mankind; or he can dwell in the planes round the earth without the physical body, helping in the further evolution of the globe and of the race.

It may partially aspire and partially tend downwards. This is the normal experience of the average man. All life is a battlefield, and the battle rages in the lower manasic region, where Manas wrestles with Kâma for empire over man. Anon aspiration conquers, the chains of sense are broken, and the lower Manas, with the radiance of its birthplace on it, soars upwards on strong wings, spurning the soil of earth. But alas! too soon the pinions tire, they flag, they flutter, they cease to beat the air; and downwards falls the royal bird whose true realm is that of the higher air, and he flutters heavily to the bog of earth once more, and Kâma chains him down.

When the period of incarnation is over, and the gateway of death closes the road of earthly life, what becomes of the lower Manas in the case we are considering?

Soon after the death of the physical body, Kâma-Manas is set free, and dwells for a while on the astral plane clothed with a body of astral matter. From this all of the manasic ray that is pure and unsoiled gradually disentangles itself, and, after a lengthy period spent on the lower levels of Devachan, it returns to its source, carrying with it such of its life-experiences as are of a nature fit for assimilation with the Higher Ego. Manas thus again becomes one during the latter part of the period which intervenes between two incarnations. The manasic Ego, brooded over by Âtma-Buddhi – the two highest principles in the human constitution, not yet considered by us – passes into the devachanic state of consciousness, resting from the weariness of the life-struggle through which it has passed. The experiences of the earth-life just closed are carried into the manasic consciousness by the lower ray withdrawn into its source. They make the devachanic state a continuation of earth-life, shorn of its sorrows, a completion of the wishes and desires of earth-life, so far as those were pure and noble. The poetic phrase that "the mind creates its own heaven" is truer than many may have imagined, for everywhere man *is* what he *thinks*, and in the devachanic state the mind is unfettered by the gross physical matter through which it works on the objective plane. The devachanic period is the time for the assimilation of life experiences, the regaining of equilibrium, ere a new journey is commenced. It is the day that succeeds the night of earth-life, the alternative of the objective manifestation. Periodicity is here, as everywhere else in nature, ebb and flow, throb and rest, the rhythm of the Universal Life. This devachanic state of consciousness lasts for a period of varying length, proportioned to the stage reached in evolution, the Devachan of the average man being said to extend over some fifteen-hundred years.

Meanwhile, that portion of the impure garment of the lower Manas which remains entangled with Kâma gives to the desire-body a somewhat confused consciousness, a broken memory of the events of the life just closed. If the emotions and passions were strong and the manasic element weak during the period of incarnation, the desire-body will be strongly energised, and will persist in its activity for a considerable length of time after the death of the physical body. It will also show a considerable amount of consciousness, as much of the manasic ray will have been overpowered by the vigorous kâmic elements, and will have remained entangled in them. If, on the other hand, the earth-life just closed was characterised my mentality and purity rather than by passion, the desire-body, being but poorly energised, will be a pale simulacrum of the person to whom it belonged, and will fade away, disintegrate and perish before any long period has elapsed.

The "spook" already mentioned will now be understood. It may show very considerable intelligence, if the manasic element be still largely present, and this will be the case with the desire-body of persons of strong animal nature and forcible though coarse intellect.For intelligence working in a very powerful kâmic personality will be exceedingly strong and energetic, though not subtle or delicate, and the spook of such a person, still further vitalised by the magnetic currents of persons yet living in the body, may show much intellectual ability of a low type. But such a spook is conscienceless, devoid of good impulses, tending towards disintegration, and communications with it can work for evil only, whether we regard them as prolonging its vitality by the currents which it sucks up from the bodies and kâmic elements of the living, or as exhausting the vitality of these living persons and polluting them with astral connections of an altogether undesirable kind.

Nor should it be forgotten that, without attending séance-rooms at all, living persons may come into objectionable contact with these kâmic spooks. As already mentioned, they are attracted to places in which the animal part of man is chiefly catered for; drinking houses, gambling saloons, brothels – all these places are full of the vilest magnetism, are very whirlpools of magnetic currents of the foulest type. These attract the spooks magnetically, and they drift to such psychic maelstroms of all that is earthly and sensual. Vivified by currents so congenial to their own, the desire-bodies become more active and potent; impregnated with the emanations of passions and desires which they can no longer physically satisfy, their magnetic current reinforce the similar currents in the live persons, action and reaction continually going on, and the animal natures of the living become more potent and less controlled by the will as they are played on by these forces of the kâmic world. Kâma-loka (from *loka,* a place, and so the place for Kâma) is a name often used to designate that plane of the astral world to which these spooks belong, and from this ray forth magnetic currents of poisonous character, as from a pest-house float out germs of disease which may take root and grow in the congenial soil of some poorly vitalised physical body.

It is very possible that many will say, on reading these statements, that Theosophy is a revival of mediaeval superstitions and will lead to imaginary terrors. Theosophy explains mediaeval superstitions, and shows the natural facts on which they were founded and from which they drew their vitality. If there are planes in nature other than the physical, no amount of reasoning will get rid of them and belief in their existence will constantly reappear; but knowledge will give them their intelligible place in the universal order, and will prevent superstition by an accurate understanding of their nature, and of the laws under which they function.And let it be remembered that persons whose consciousness is normally on the physical plane can protect themselves from undesirable influences by keeping their minds clean and their wills strong. We protect ourselves best against disease by maintaining our bodies in vigorous health; we cannot guard ourselves against invisible germs, but we can prevent our bodies from becoming suitable soil for the growth and development of the germs. Nor need we deliberately throw ourselves in the way infection. So also as regards these malign germs from the astral plane. We can prevent the formation of Kâma-manasic soil in which they can germinate and develop, and we need not go into evil places, nor deliberately encourage receptivity and mediumistic tendencies. A strong active will and a pure heart are our best protection.

There remains the third possibility for Kâma-Manas, to which we must now turn our attention, the fate spoken of earlier as "terrible in its consequences, which may befall the kâmic principle".

It may break away from its source made one with Kâma instead of with the higher Manas. This is fortunately, a rare event, as rare at one pole of human life as the complete re-union with the higher Manas is rare at the other. But still the possibility remains and must be stated.

The personality may be so strongly controlled by Kâma that, in the struggle between the kâmic and manasic elements, the victory may remain wholly with the former. The lower Manas may become so enslaved that its essence may be frayed and thinner and thinner by the constant rub and strain, until at last persistent yielding to the promptings of desire bears its inevitable fruit, and the slender link which unites the higher to the lower Manas, the "silver thread that binds it to the Master", snaps in two. Then, during earth-life, the lower quaternary is wrenched away from the Triad to which it was linked, and the higher nature is severed wholly from the lower. The human being is rent in twain, the brute has broken itself free, and it goes forth unbridled, carrying with it the reflections of that manasic light which should have been its guide through the desert of life. A more dangerous brute it is than its fellows of the unevolved animal world, just because of these fragments in it of the higher mentality of man. Such a being, human in form but brute in nature, human in appearance but without human truth, or love or justice – such a one may now and then be met with in the haunts of men, putrescent while still living, a thing to shudder at with deepest, if hopeless compassion. What is its fate after the funeral knell has tolled?

Ultimately, there is the perishing of the personality that has thus broken away from the principles that can alone give it immortality. But a period of persistence lies before it.

The desire-body of such a one is an entity of terrible potency, and it has this unique peculiarity, that it is able under certain rare circumstances to reincarnate in the world of men. It is not a mere "spook" on the way to disintegration; it has retained, entangled in its coils, too much of the manasic element to permit of such natural dissipation in space. It is sufficiently an independent entity, lurid instead of radiant, with manasic flame rendered foul instead of purifying, as to be able to take to itself a garment of flesh once more and dwell as man with men. Such a man – if the word may indeed be applied to the mere human shell with brute interior – passes through a period of earth-life the natural foe of all who are still normal in their humanity. With no instincts save those of the animal, driven only by passion, never even by emotion, with a cunning that no brute can rival, a deliberate wickedness that plans evil in fashion unknown to the mere frankly natural impulses of the animal world, the reincarnated entity touches ideal vileness. Such soil the page of human history as the monsters of iniquity that startle us now and again into a wondering cry, "Is this a human being?" Sinking lower with each successive incarnation, the evil force gradually wears itself out, and such a personality perishes separated from the source of life. It finally disintegrates, to be worked up into other forms of living things, but as a separate existence, it is lost. It is a bead broken off the thread of life, and the immortal Ego that incarnated in that personality has lost the experience of that incarnation, has reaped no harvest from that life-sowing. Its ray has brought nothing back, its lifework for that birth has been a total and complete failure, whereof nothing remains to weave into the fabric of its own eternal Self.

SUBTLE FORMS OF THE FOURTH AND FIFTH PRINCIPLE

The student will already have fully realised that "an astral body" is a loose term that may cover a variety of different forms. It may be well at this stage to sum up the subtle types sometimes inaccurately called the astral that belong to the fourth and fifth principles.

During life a true astral body may be projected – formed, as its name implies, of astral matter – but, unlike the etheric double, dowered with intelligence, and able to travel to a considerable distance from the physical body to which it belongs. This is the desire-body, and it is, as we have seen, a vehicle of consciousness. It is projected by mediums and sensitives unconsciously, and by trained students consciously. It can travel with the speed of thought to a distant place, can there gather impressions from surrounding objects, can bring back those impressions to the physical body. In the case of a medium it can convey them to others by means of the physical body still entranced, but as a rule when the sensitive comes out of trance, the brain does not retain the impressions thus made upon it, and no trace is left in the memory of the experiences thus acquired. Sometimes, but this is rare, the desire-body is able sufficiently to affect the brain by the vibrations it set up, to leave a lasting impression thereon, and then the sensitive is able to recall the knowledge acquired during trance. The student learns to impress on his brain the knowledge gained in the desire-body, his will being active while that of the medium is passive.

This desire-body is the agent unconsciously used by clairvoyants when their vision is not merely the seeing in the astral light. This astral form does then really travel to distant places, and may appear there to persons who are sensitive or who chance for the time to be in an abnormal nervous condition. Sometimes it appears to them – when very faintly informed by consciousness – as a vaguely outlined form, not noticing its surroundings. Such a body has appeared near the time of death at places distant from the dying person, to those who were closely united to the dying by ties of the blood, of affection, or of hatred. More highly energised, it will show intelligence and emotion, as in some cases on record, in which dying mothers have visited their children residing at a distance, and have spoken in their last moments of what they had seen and done. The desire-body is also set free in many cases of disease – as is the etheric double – as well as in sleep and in trance. Inactivity of the physical body is a condition of such astral voyagings.

The desire-body seems also occasionally to appear in séance-rooms, giving rise to some of the more intellectual phenomena that takes place. It must not be confounded with the "spook" already sufficiently familiar to the reader, the latter being always the kâmic or Kâma-Manasic remains of some dead person, whereas the body we are now dealing with is the projection of an astral double from a living person.

A higher form of subtle body, belonging to Manas, is that known as the Mâyâvi Rûpa, or "body of illusion". The Mâyâvi Rûpa is a subtle body formed by the consciously directed will of the Adept or disciple; it may, or may not, resemble the physical body, the form given to it being suitable to the purpose for which it is projected. In this body the full consciousness dwells, for it is merely the mental body rearranged. The Adept or disciple can thus travel at will, without the burden of the physical body, in the full exercise of every faculty, in perfect self-consciousness. He makes the Mâyâvi Rûpa visible of invisible at will – on the physical plane – and the phrase often used by chelâs and others as to seeing an Adept "in his astral", means that he was visited by them in his Mâyâvi Rûpa. If he so chose, he can make it, indistinguishable from a physical body, warm and firm to the touch as well as visible, able to carry on a conversation, at all points like a physical human being. But the power thus to form the true Mâyâvi Rûpa is confined to Adepts and chelâs; it cannot be done by the untrained student, however psychic he may naturally be, for it is a manasic and not a psychic creation, and it is only under the instruction of his Guru that the chelâ learns to form and use the "body of illusion".

THE HIGHER MANAS

The immortal Thinker itself, as will by this time have become clear to the reader, can manifest itself but little on the physical plane at the present stage of human evolution. Yet we are able to catch some glimpses of the powers resident in it, the more as in the lower Manas we find those powers "cribbed, cabined and confined" indeed, but yet existing. Thus we have seen that the lower Manas "is the organ of the freewill in physical man". Freewill resides in Manas itself, in Manas the representative of Mahat, the Universal Mind. From Manas comes the feeling of liberty, the knowledge that we can rule ourselves – really the knowledge that the higher nature in us can rule the lower, let that lower nature rebel and struggle as it may. Once let our consciousness identify itself with Manas instead of with Kâma, and the lower nature becomes the animal we bestride, it is no longer the "I". All its plungings, its struggles, its fights for mastery, are then outside us, not within us, and we rein it in and hold it as we rein in a plunging steed and subdue it to our will.

On this question of freewill I venture to quote from an article of my own that appeared in the *Path* –

"Unconditioned will, alone can be absolutely free: the unconditioned and the absolute are one: all that is conditioned must, by virtue of that conditioning, be relative and therefore partially bound. As that will evolves the universe, it becomes conditioned by the laws of its own manifestation. The manasic entities are differentiations of that will, each conditioned by the nature of its manifesting potency, but, while conditioned without, it is free within its own sphere of activity, so being the image in its own world of the universal will in the universe. Now as this will, acting on each successive plane, crystalises itself more and more densely as matter, the manifestation is conditioned by the material in which it works, while, relatively to the material, it is itself free. So at each stage the inner freedom appears in consciousness, while yet investigation shows that, that freedom works within the limits of the plane of manifestation on which it is acting, free to work upon the lower, yet hindered as to manifestation by the unresponsiveness of the lower to its impulse. Thus the higher Manas, in whom resides free will, so far as the lower quaternary is concerned – being the offspring of Mahat, the third Logos, the Word, *i.e.,* the Will in manifestation – is limited in its manifestation in our lower nature by the sluggishness of the response of the personality to its impulses. In the lower Manas itself – as immersed in that personality - resides the will with which we are familiar, swayed by passions, by appetites, by desires, by impressions coming from without, yet able to assert itself among them all, by virtue of its essential nature, one with that higher Ego of which it is the ray. It is free, as regards all below it, able to act on Kâma and on the physical body, however much its full expression may be thwarted and hindered by the crudeness of the material in which it is working. Were the will the mere outcome of the physical body, of the desires and passions, whence could arise the sense of the "I" that can judge, can desire, can overcome? It acts from a higher plane, is royal as touching the lower whenever it claims the royalty of birthright, and the very struggle of its self-assertion is the best testimony to the fact that in its nature it is free. And so, passing to lower planes, we find in each grade this freedom of the higher as ruling the lower, yet, on the plane of the lower, hindered in manifestation . Reversing the process and starting from the lower, the same truth becomes manifest. Let a man's limbs be loaded with fetters, and crude material iron will prevent the manifestation of the muscular and nervous force with which they are instinct: none the less is that force present, though hindered for the moment in its activity. Its strength may be shown in its very efforts to break the chains that bind it there, is no power in the iron to prevent the free giving out of the muscular energy, though the phenomena of motion may be hindered. But while this energy cannot be ruled by the physical nature below, its expenditure is determined by the kâmic principle; passions and desires can set it going, can direct and control it. The muscular and nervous energy cannot rule the passions and desires, they are free as regards it, it is determined by their interposition. Yet again Kâma may be ruled, controlled, determined by the will; as touching the manasic principle it is bound, not free, and hence the sense of freedom in choosing which desire shall be gratified, which act performed. As the lower Manas rules Kâma, the lower quaternary takes its rightful position of subserviency to the higher triad, and is determined by a will it recognises as above itself, and, as it regards itself, a will that is free. Here in many a mind will spring the question, 'And what of the will of the higher Manas; is that in turn determined by what is above it, while it is free to all below? But we have reached a point where the intellect fails us, and where language may not easily utter that which the Spirit senses in those higher realms. Dimly only can we feel that there, as everywhere else, "the truest freedom must be in harmony with law, and that voluntary acceptance of the function of acting as channel of the Universal Will must unite into one perfect liberty and perfect obedience".

This is truly an obscure and difficult problem, but the student will find much light fall on it by following the lines of thought thus traced.

Another power resident in the higher Manas and manifested on the lower planes by those in whom the higher Manas is consciously master, is that of creation of forms by the will. The *Secret Doctrine* says: "Kriyashakti". The mysterious power of thought which enables it to produce external, perceptible, phenomenal results by its own inherent energy. The ancient held that *any idea will manifest itself externally if one's attention is deeply concentrated upon it. Similarly an intense volition will be followed by the desired results"*. Here is the secret of true "magic". and as the subject is an important one, and as Western science is beginning to touch its fringe, a separate section is devoted to its consideration farther on, in order not to break the connected outline here given on principles.

Again we have learned from H.P.Blavatsky that Manas, or the higher Ego, as "part of the essence of the Universal Mind, is unconditionally omniscient on its own plane", when it has fully developed self-consciousness by its evolutionary experiences, and "is the vehicle of all knowledge of the past and present, and the future". When this immortal entity is able through its ray, the lower Manas, to impress the brain of a man, that man is one who manifests abnormal qualities, is a genius or seer. The conditions of seership are thus laid down:

"The former [the visions of the true seer] can be obtained by one of two means: (a) on the condition of paralysing at will the *memory* and the instinctual independent action of all the material organs and even cells in the body of flesh, an act which, when once the light of the higher Ego has consumed and subjected for ever the passional nature of the personal lower Ego, is easy, but requires an adept; (b) of being a reincarnation of one who, in a previous birth, had attained through extreme purity of life and efforts in the right direction almost to a Yogi-state of holiness and saintship. There is also a third possibility of reaching in mystic visions the plane of the higher Manas; but it is only occasional, and does not depend on the will of the seer, but on the extreme weakness and exhaustion of the material body through illness and suffering. The Seeress of Prevorst was an instance of the latter case; and Jacob Boehme of our second category".

The reader will now be in a position to grasp the difference between the workings of the higher Ego and of its ray. Genius, which *sees* instead of arguing, is of the higher Ego; true intuition is one of its faculties. Reason, the weighing and balancing quality which arranges the facts gathered by observation, balances them one against the other, argues from them, draws conclusions from them – this is the exercise of the lower Manas through the brain apparatus; its instrument is ratiocination; by induction it ascends from the known to the unknown, building up a hypothesis; by deduction it descends again to the known, verifying its hypothesis by fresh experiment.

Intuition, as we see by its derivation, is simply insight – a process as direct and swift as bodily vision. It is the exercise of the eyes of the intelligence, the unerring recognition of a truth presented on the mental plane. It sees with certainty, its vision is unclouded, its report unfaltering. No proof can add to the certitude of its recognition, for it is beyond and above the reason . Often our instincts, blinded and confused by passions and desires, are miscalled intuitions, and a mere kâmic impulse is accepted as the sublime voice of the higher Manas. Careful and prolonged self-training is necessary, ere the voice can be recognised with certainty, but of one thing we may feel very sure: so long as we are in the vortex of the personality, so long as the storms of desires and appetites howl around us, so long as the waves of emotion toss us to and fro, so long the voice of the higher Manas cannot reach our ears. Not in the fire or the whirlwind, not in the thunderclap of the storm, comes the mandate of the higher Ego: only when there has fallen the stillness of a silence that can be felt, only when the very air is motionless and the calm is profound, only when the man wraps his face in a mantle which closes his ears even to the silence that is of earth, then only sounds the voice that is stiller than the silence, the voice of his true Self.

On this H. P. Blavatsky has written in *Isis Unveiled*: "Allied to the physical half of man's nature is reason, which enables him to maintain his supremacy over the lower animals, and to subjugate nature to his uses. Allied to his spiritual part is his conscience, which will serve as his unerring guide through the besetment of the senses; for conscience is that instantaneous perception between right and wrong which can only be exercised by the spirit, which, being a portion of the divine wisdom and purity, is absolutely pure and wise.Its promptings are independent of reason, and it can only manifest itself clearly when unhampered by the baser attractions of our dual nature. Reason being a faculty of our physical brain, one which is justly defined as that of deducing inferences from premises, and being wholly dependent on the evidence of other senses, cannot be a quality pertaining directly to our divine spirit. The latter *knows* – hence all reasoning, which implies discussion and argument, would be useless. So an entity which, if it must be considered as a direct emanation from the eternal Spirit of wisdom, has to be vied as possessed of the same attributes as the essence of the whole of which it is part. Therefore it is with a certain degree of logic that the ancient Theurgists maintained that the rational part of a man's soul (spirit) never entered wholly into the man's body, but only overshadowed him more or less through the irrational or astral soul, which serves as an intermediary agent, or a medium between spirit and body.The man who has conquered matter sufficiently to receive the direct light from his shining *Augoeides,* feels truth intuitively; he could not err in his judgement, notwithstanding all the sophisms suggested by cold reason, for he is *illuminated.* Hence prophesy, vaticination, and the so-called divine inspiration, are simply the effects of this illumination from above by our own immortal spirit".

This Augoeides, according to the belief of the Neo-Platonists, as according to the Theosophical teachings, "sheds more or less its radiance on the inner man, the astral soul" *i.e..,* in the now accepted terminology, on the Kâma-Manasic personality or lower Ego. (In reading *Isis Unveiled*, the student has to bear in mind the fact that when the book was written, the terminology was by no means even as fixed as it is now; in *Isis Unveiled* is the first modern attempt to translate into Western language the complicated Eastern ideas, and further experience has shown that many of the terms used to cover two or three conceptions may with advantage be restricted to one and thus rendered precise. Thus the "astral soul" must be understood in the sense given above.) Only as this lower Ego becomes pure from all breath of passion, as the lower Manas frees itself from Kâma, can the "shining one" impress it; H.P. Blavatsky tells how initiates meet this higher Ego face to face. Having spoken of the trinity in man, Âtma-Buddhi-Manas, she goes on: "It is when this trinity, in anticipation of the final triumphant reunion beyond the gates of corporeal death, became for a few seconds a unity, that the candidate is allowed, at the moment of the initiation, to behold his future self. Thus we read in the Persian *Desatir* of the 'resplendent one'; in the Greek philosopher-initiates of the Augoeides – the self-shining 'blessed vision resident in the pure light'; in Porphyry, that Plotinus was united to his 'god' six times during his lifetime, and so on".

This trinity made into unity, again, is the "Christ" of all mystics. When in the final initiation, the candidate has been outstretched on the floor or altar stone and has thus typified the crucifixion of the flesh, or lower nature, and when from this "death" he has "risen again" as the triumphant conqueror over sin and death, he then, in the supreme moment, sees before him the glorious presence and becomes "one with Christ," is himself the Christ. Thenceforth he may live in the body, but it has become his obedient instrument; he is united with his true Self, Manas made one with Âtma-Buddhi, and through the personality which he inhabits he wields his full powers as an immortal spiritual intelligence. While he was still struggling in the toils of the lower nature, Christ, the spiritual Ego, was daily crucified in him; but in the full Adept Christ has arisen triumphant, lord of himself and of nature. The long pilgrimage of Manas is over, the cycle of necessity is trodden, the wheel of rebirth ceases to turn, the Son of man has been made perfect by suffering.

So long as this point has not been reached, "the Christ" is the object of aspiration. The ray is ever struggling to return to its source, the lower Manas ever aspiring to re-become one with the higher. While this duality persists the continual yearning towards reunion felt by the noblest and purest natures is one of the most salient facts of the inner life, and it is this which clothes itself as prayer, as inspiration, as "seeking after God," as the longing for union with the divine. "My soul is athirst for God, for the living God", cries the eager Christian, and to tell him that this intense longing is a fancy and is futile to make him turn aside from you as one who cannot understand, but whose insensibility does not alter the fact. The Occultist recognises in this cry the inextinguishable impulse upwards of the lower Self to the higher from which it is separated, but the attraction of which it vividly feels. Whether the person pray to the Buddha, to Vishnu, to Christ, to the Virgin, to the Father, it matters not at all; these are questions of mere dialect, not of essential fact. In all the Manas united to Âtma-Buddhi is the real object, veiled under what name the changing time or race may give; at once the ideal humanity and the "personal God", the "God Man" found in all religions, "God incarnate", the "Word made flesh", "the Christ who must be born in each", with whom the believer must be made one.

And this leads us on to the last planes with which we are concerned, the planes of Spirit, using that much abused word merely as the opposite pole to matter; here only very general ideas can be grasped by us, but it is necessary none the less to try to grasp these ideas if we are to complete, however poorly our conception of man.

PRINCIPLES SIX AND SEVEN
ÂTMA – BUDDHI, THE SPIRIT

As the completion of the thought of the last section, we will look at Âtma-Buddhi first in its connection with Manas, and will then proceed to a somewhat more general view of it as the "Monad." The clearest and best description of the human trinity, Âtma-Buddhi-Manas, will be found in the *Key to Theosophy*, in which H.P.Blavatsky gives the following definitions:

THE HIGHER SELF is	*Atma,* the inseparable ray of the Universal and ONE SELF. It is the God *above*, more than within us. Happy the man who succeeds in saturating his *inner Ego* with it
THE SPIRITUAL *divine* EGO is	the spiritual soul, or *Buddhi,* in close union with *Manas,* the mind-principle, without which it is no EGO at all, but only the Atmic Vehicle.
THE INNER or HIGHER EGO is	*Manas,* the fifth principle, so called, independently of Buddhi. The mind-principle is only the Spiritual Ego when merged into one with Buddhi .. It is the permanent individuality or the reincarnating Ego.

Âtmâ must then be regarded as the most abstract part of man's nature, the "breath" which needs a body for its manifestation. It is the one reality, that which manifests on all planes, the essence of which all our principles are but aspects. The one Eternal Existence, wherefrom are all things, which embodies one of its aspects in the universe, that which we speak of as the One Life – this Eternal Existence rays forth as Âtmâ, the very Self alike of the universe and of man; their innermost core, their very heart, that in which all things inhere. In itself incapable of direct manifestation on lower planes, yet That without which no lower planes could come into existence, It clothes Itself in Buddhi, as Its vehicle, or medium of further manifestation. "Buddhi is the faculty of cognising, the channel through which divine knowledge reaches the Ego, the discernment of good and evil, also divine conscience, and the spiritual Soul, which is the vehicle of Âtmâ". It is often spoken of as the principle of spiritual discernment. But Âtma-Buddhi, a universal principle, needs individualising ere experience can be gathered and self-consciousness attained. So the mind-principle is united to Âtma-Buddhi, and the human trinity is complete. Manas becomes the *spiritual* Ego only when merged in Buddhi; Buddhi becomes the spiritual *Ego* only when united to Manas; in the union of the two lies the evolution of the Spirit, self-conscious on all planes. Hence Manas strives upward to Âtma-Buddhi, as the lower Manas strives upward to the higher, and hence, in relation to the higher Manas, Âtma-Buddhi, or Âtma, is often spoken of as "the Father in Heaven", as the higher Manas is itself thus described in relation to the lower. The lower Manas gathers experience to carry it back to its source; the higher Manas accumulates the store throughout the cycle of reincarnation; Buddhi becomes assimilated with the higher Manas; and these, permeated with the Âtmic light, one with that True Self, the trinity becomes a unity, the Spirit is self-conscious on all planes, and the object of the manifested universe is attained.

But no words of mine can avail to explain or to describe that which is beyond explanation and beyond description. Words can but blunder along on such a theme, dwarfing and distorting it. Only by long and patient meditation can the student hope vaguely to sense something greater than himself, yet something which stirs at the innermost core of his being. As to the steady gaze directed at the pale evening sky, there appears after while, faintly and far away, the soft glimmer of a star, so to the patient gaze of the inner vision there may come the tender beam of the spiritual star, if but as a mere suggestion of a far off world. Only to a patient and persevering purity will that light arise, and blessed beyond all earthly blessedness is he who sees but the palest shimmer of that transcendent radiance.

With such ideas as to "Spirit", the horror with which Theosophists shrink from ascribing the trivial phenomena of the séance-room to "spirits" will be readily understood. Playing on musical boxes, talking through trumpets, tapping people on the head, carrying accordions round the room – these things may be all very well for astrals, spooks and elementals, but who can assign them to "spirits", who has any conception of Spirit worthy of the name? Such vulgarisation and degradation of the most sublime conceptions as yet evolved by man are surely subjects for the keenest regret, and it may well be hoped that ere long these phenomena will be put in their true place, as evidence that the materialistic views of the universe are inadequate, instead of being exalted to a place they cannot fill as proofs of Spirit. No physical, no intellectual phenomena are proofs of the existence of Spirit. Only to the spirit can Spirit be demonstrated. You cannot prove a proposition in Euclid to a dog; you cannot prove Âtma-Buddhi to Kâma and the lower Manas. As we climb, our view will widen, and when we stand on the summit of the Holy Mount the planes of Spirit shall lie before our opened vision.

THE MONAD IN EVOLUTION

Perhaps a slightly more definite conception of Atmâ-Buddhi may be obtained by the student, if he considers its work in evolution as the Monad. Now Atmâ-Buddhi is identical with the universal Over-soul , "itself an aspect of the Unknown Root", the One Existence. When manifestation begins the Monad is "thrown downwards into matter", to propel forward and force evolution (See *Secret Doctrine,* Volume 2, page 115); it is the mainspring, so to speak, of all evolution, the impelling force at the root of all things. All the principles we have been studying are mere "variously differentiated aspects" of Atmâ, the One Reality manifesting in our universe; it is in every atom, "the root of every atom individually and of every form collectively", and all the principles are fundamentally Atmâ on different planes. The stages of its evolution are very clearly laid down in *Five Years of Theosophy.* There we are shown how it passes through the stages termed elemental, "nascent centres of forces", and reaches the mineral stage; from this it passes up through vegetable, animal, to man, vivifying every form. As we are taught in the *Secret Doctrine*: "The well-known Kabbalistic aphorism runs:

"A stone becomes a plant; the plant a beast; the beast, a man; the man, a spirit; and the spirit, a god."

The 'spark' animates all the kingdoms in turn before it enters into and informs divine man, between whom and his predecessor, animal man, there is all the difference in the world….The Monad…is first of all, shot down by the law of evolution into the lowest form of matter – the mineral. After a sevenfold gyration incased in the stone, or that which will become mineral and stone in the Fourth Round, it creeps out of it, say as a lichen. Passing thence, through all the forms of vegetable matter, into what is termed animal matter, it has now reached the point in which it has become the germ, so to speak, of the animal, that will become the physical man".

It is the Monad, Âtma-Buddhi, that thus vivifies every part and kingdom of nature, making all instinct with life and consciousness, one throbbing whole. "Occultism does not accept anything inorganic in the Kosmos. The expression employed by science, ' inorganic substance,' means simply that the latent life, slumbering in the molecules of so-called 'inert matter,' is incognisable. All is life and every atom of even mineral dust is a life, though beyond our comprehension and perception, because it is outside the range of the laws known to those who reject Occultism "(*Secret Doctrine*, Vol. I, pages 268-69). And again: "Everything in the universe, throughout all its kingdoms, is conscious, *i.e..,* endowed with a consciousness of its own kind and on its own plane of perception. We men must remember that simply because *we* do not perceive any signs of consciousness which we can recognise, say in stones, we have no right to say that no consciousness exists there. There is no such thing as either 'dead' or 'blind' matter, as there is no 'blind' or 'unconscious' law".

How many of the great poets, with the sublime intuition of genius, have sensed this great truth! To them all nature pulses with life; they see life and love everywhere, in suns and planets as in the grains of dust, in rustling leaves and opening blossoms, in dancing gnats and gliding snakes. Each form manifests as much of the One Life as it is capable of expressing, and what is man that he should despise the more limited manifestations, when he compares himself as a life-expression, not with the forms below him, but with the possibilities of expression that soar above him in infinite heights of being, which he can estimate still less than the stone can estimate him?

The student will readily see that we must regard this force at the centre of evolution as essentially *one*. There is but one Âtma-Buddhi in our universe, the universal Soul, everywhere present, immanent in all, the One Supreme Energy whereof all varying energies or forces are only differing forms. As the sunbeam is light or heat or electricity according to its conditioning environment, so is Âtma all-energy, differentiating on different planes. "As an abstraction, we will call it the One Life; as an objective and evident reality, we speak of a septenary scale of manifestation, which begins at the upper rung with the one unknowable causality, and ends as Omnipresent Mind and Life immanent in every atom of matter".

Its evolutionary course is very plainly outlined in a quotation given in the *Secret Doctrine*, and as students are very often puzzled over this unity of the Monad, I subjoin the statement. The subject is difficult, but it could not, I think, be more clearly put than it is in these sentences:

"Now the monadic or cosmic essence (if such a term be permitted) in the mineral, vegetable, and animal, though the same throughout the series of cycles from the lowest elemental up to the Deva kingdom, yet differs in the scale of progression. It would be very misleading to imagine a Monad as a separate entity trailing its slow way in a distinct path through the lower kingdoms, and after incalculable series of transformations flowering into a human being; in short, that the Monad of a Humboldt dates back to the Monad of an atom of hornblende. Instead of saying a 'Mineral Monad,' the more correct phraseology in physical science, which differentiates every atom, would of course have been to call it 'the Monad manifesting in that form of Prakriti called the mineral kingdom.' The atom, as represented in the ordinary scientific hypothesis, is not a particle of something, animated by a psychic something, destined after aeons to blossom as a man. But it is a concrete manifestation of the universal energy which itself has not yet become individualised; a sequential manifestation of the one universal Monad The ocean of matter does not divide into its potential and constituent drops until the sweep of the life-impulse reaches the stage of man-birth. The tendency towards segregation into individual Monads is gradual, and in the higher animals comes almost to the point. The Peripatetics applied the word Monad to the whole Kosmos in the pantheistic sense; and the Occultists, while accepting this thought for convenience sake, distinguish the progressive stages of the evolution of the concrete from the abstract by terms of which the 'mineral, vegetable, animal, Monad,' etc., are examples. The term merely means that the tidal wave of spiritual evolution is passing through that arc of its circuit. The 'Monadic Essence' begins imperfectly to differentiate towards individual consciousness in the vegetable kingdom. As the Monads are un-compounded things, as correctly defined by Leibnitz, it is the spiritual essence which vivifies them in their degrees of differentiation, which properly constitutes the Monad – not the atomic aggregation, which is only the vehicle and the substance through which thrill the lower and the higher degrees of intelligence".

The student who reads and weighs this passage will, at the cost of a little present trouble, save himself from much confusion in days to come. Let him first realise clearly that the Monad – "the spiritual essence" to which alone in strict accuracy the term Monad should be applied – is *one* all the universe over, that Âtma-Buddhi is not his, nor mine, nor the property of anybody in particular, but the spiritual essence energising in all. So is electricity *one* all the world over; though it may be active in his machine or in mine, neither he nor I can call it distinctly our electricity. But – and here arise confusion – when Âtma-Buddhi energises in man, in whom Manas is active as an individualising force, it is often spoken of as though the "atomic aggregation" were a separate Monad, and then we have "Monads," as in the above passage. This loose way of using the word will not lead to error if the student will remember that the individualising process *is not on the spiritual plane*, but Âtma-Buddhi *as seen through Manas* seems to share in the individuality of the latter. So if you hold pieces of variously coloured glass in your hand you may see through them a red sun, a blue sun, a yellow sun, and so on. None the less there is only the one sun shining down upon you, altered by the media through which you look at it. So we often meet the phrase "human Monads"; it should be "the Monad manifesting in the human kingdom"; but this somewhat pedantic accuracy would be likely only to puzzle a large number of people, and the looser popular phrase will not mislead when the principle of the unity on the spiritual plane is grasped, any more than we mislead by speaking of the rising of the sun. "The Spiritual Monad is one, universal, boundless, and impartite, whose rays, nevertheless, form what we, in our ignorance, call the ' individual Monads' of men".

Very beautifully and poetically is this unity in diversity put in one of the Occult Catechisms in which the Guru questions the Chela:

"Lift thy head, O Lanoo; dost thou see one or countless lights above thee, burning in the dark midnight sky?"

"I sense one Flame, O Gurudeva; I see countless undetached sparks burning in it."

"Thou sayest well. And now look around and into thyself. That light which burns inside thee, dost thou feel it different in any wise from the light that shines in thy brother-men?"

"It is in no way different, though the prisoner is held in bondage by Karma, and though its outer garments delude the ignorant into saying, 'thy soul' and 'my soul'".

There ought not to be any serious difficulty now in grasping the stages of human evolution; the Monad, which has been working its way as we have seen, reaches the point at which the human form can be built up on earth; an etheric body and its physical counterpart are then developed, Prâna specialised from the great ocean of life, and Kâma evolved, all these principles, the lower quaternary, being brooded over by the Monad, energised by it, impelled by it, forced onward by it towards continually increasing perfection of form and capacity for manifesting the higher energies in Nature. This was animal, or physical man, evolved through two and a half Races. But the Monad and the lower quaternary could not come into sufficiently close relation with each other; a link was yet wanting. "The Double Dragon [the Monad] has no hold upon the mere form. It is like the breeze where there is no tree or branch to receive and harbour it. It cannot affect the form where there is no agent of transmission, and the form knows it not. Then, at the middle point just reached, in the middle, that is, of the Third race, the lower Mânasaputra stepped in to inhabit the dwellings thus prepared for them, and to form the bridge between animal man and the Spirit, between the evolved quaternary and the brooding Âtma-Buddhi, to begin the long cycle of reincarnation which is to issue in the perfect man.

The "monadic inflow," or the evolution of the Monad, from the animal into the human kingdom, continued through the Third Race on to the middle of the Fourth, the human population thus continually receiving fresh recruits, the birth of souls thus continuing through the second half of the Third race and the first half of the Fourth. After this, the "central turning point" of the cycle of evolution, "no more Monads can enter the human kingdom. The door is closed for this cycle". Since then reincarnation has been the method of evolution, this individual reincarnation of the immortal Thinker in conjunction with Âtma-Buddhi replacing the collective indwelling of Âtma-Buddhi in lower forms of matter.

According to Theosophical teachings, humanity has now reached the Fifth Race, and we are in the fifth sub-race thereof, mankind on this globe in the present stage having before it the completion of the Fifth race, and the rise, maturity and decay of the Sixth and Seventh Races. But during all the ages necessary for this evolution, there is no increase in the total number of reincarnating Egos; only a small proportion of these are reincarnated at any special time on our globe, so that the population may ebb and flow within very wide limits, and it will have been noticed that there is a rush of birth after a local depopulation has been caused by exceptional mortality. There is room and to spare for all such fluctuations, having in view the difference between the total number of reincarnating Egos and the number actually incarnated at a given period.

LINES OF PROOF FOR AN UNTRAINED ENQUIRER

It is natural and right that any thoughtful person brought face to face with assertions such as those put forth in the preceding pages, should demand what proof is forthcoming to substantiate the propositions laid down. A reasonable person will not demand full and complete proof available to all comers, without study and without painstaking. He will admit that the advanced theories of a science cannot be demonstrated to one ignorant of its first principles, and he will be prepared to find that very much will have been alleged which can only be proved to those who have made some progress in their study. An essay on the higher mathematics, on the correlation of forces, on the atomic theory, on the molecular constitution of chemical compounds, would contain many statements the proofs of which would only be available for those who had devoted time and thought to the study of the elements of the science concerned; and so an unprejudiced person, confronted with the Theosophical view of the constitution of man, would readily admit that he could not expect complete demonstration until he had mastered the elements of the Theosophical science.

None the less are there general proofs available in every science which suffice to justify its existence and to encourage study of its more recondite truths; and in Theosophy it is possible to indicate lines of proof which can be followed by the untrained enquirer, and which justify him in devoting time and pains to a study which gives promise of a wider and deeper knowledge of himself and of external nature than is otherwise attainable.

It is well to say at the outset that there is no proof available to the average enquirer of the existence of the three higher planes of which we have spoken. The realms of Spirit, and of the higher mind are closed to all save those who have evolved the faculties necessary for their investigation. Those who have evolved these faculties need no proof of the existence of those realms; to those who have not, no proof of their existence can be given. That there is *something* above the astral and the lower levels of the mental plane may indeed be proved by the flashes of genius, the lofty intuitions, that from time to time lighten the darkness of our lower world; but what that something is, only those can say whose inner eyes have been opened, who see where the race as a whole is still blind. But the lower planes are susceptible to proof, and fresh proofs are accumulating day be day. The Masters of Wisdom are using the investigators and thinkers of the Western world to make "discoveries" which tend to substantiate the outposts of the Theosophical position, and the lines which they are following are

53

exactly those which are needed for the finding of natural laws which will justify the assertions of Theosophists with regard to the elementary "powers" and "phenomena" to which such exaggerated importance has been given. If it is found that we have undeniable facts which establish the existence of planes other than the physical on which consciousness can work; which establish the existence of senses and powers of perception other than those with which we are familiar in daily life; which establish the existence of powers of communication between intelligences without the use of mechanical apparatus, surely, under these circumstances, the Theosophist may claim that he has made out a *prima facie* case for further investigation of his doctrines.

Let us then, confine ourselves to the lower planes of which we have spoken in the preceding pages, and the four lower principles in man which are correlated with these planes. Of these four, we may dismiss one, that of Prâna, as none will challenge the fact of the existence of the energy we call "life"; the need of isolating it for purposes of study may be challenged, and in very truth the plane of Prâna, or the principle of Prâna, runs through all other planes, all other principles, interpenetrating all and binding all in one. There remain for our study the physical plane, the astral plane, the lower levels of the manasic plane. Can we substantiate these by proofs which will be accepted by those who are not yet Theosophists? I think we can.

First, as regards the physical plane. We need here to notice how the senses of man are correlated with the physical universe outside him, and how his knowledge of that universe is bounded by the power of his organs of sense to vibrate in response to vibrations set up outside him. He can hear when the air is thrown into vibrations into which the drum of his ear can also be thrown; if the vibration be so slow that the drum cannot vibrate in answer, the person does not hear any sound; if the vibration be so rapid that the drum cannot vibrate in answer, the person does not hear any sound. So true is this, that the limit of hearing in different persons varies with this power of vibration of the drums of their respective ears; one person is plunged in silence, while another is deafened by the keen shrilling that is throwing into tumult the air around both. The same principle holds good for sight; we see so long as the light waves are of a length to which our organs of sight can respond; below and beyond this length we are in darkness, let the ether vibrate as it may. The ant can see where we are blind, because its eye can receive and respond to etheric vibrations more rapid than we can sense.

All this suggests to any thoughtful person the idea that if our senses could be evolved to more responsiveness, new avenues of knowledge would be opened up even on the physical plane; this realised, it is not difficult to go a step farther, and to conceive that keener and subtler senses might exist which would open up, as it were, a new universe on a plane other than the physical.

Now this conception is true, and with the evolution of the astral senses the astral plane unfolds itself, and may be studied as really, as scientifically, as the physical universe can be. These astral senses exist in all men, but are latent in most, and generally need to be artificially forced, if they are to be used in the present stage of evolution. In a few persons they are normally present and become active without any artificial impulse. In very many persons they can be artificially awakened and developed. The condition, in all cases, of the activity of the astral senses is the passivity of the physical, and the more complete passivity on the physical plane the greater the possibility of activity on the astral.

It is noteworthy that Western psychologists have found it necessary to investigate what is termed the "dream consciousness", in order to understand the workings of consciousness as a whole. It is impossible to ignore the strange phenomena which characterise the workings of consciousness when it is removed from the limitations of the physical plane, and some of the most able and advanced of our psychologists do not think these workings to be in any way unworthy of the most careful and scientific investigation. All such workings are, in Theosophical language, on the astral plane, and the student who seeks for proof there is an astral plane may here find enough and to spare. He will speedily discover that the laws under which consciousness works on the physical plane have no existence on the astral. E.g., the laws of space and time, which are here the very conditions of thought, do not exist for consciousness when its activity is transferred to the astral world. Mozart hears a whole symphony as a single impression, "as in a fine and strong dream", but has to work it out in successive details when he brings it back with him to the physical plane. The dream of the moment contains a mass of events that would take years to pass in succession in our world of space and time. The drowning man sees his life history in a few seconds. But it is needless to multiply instances.

The astral plane may be reached in sleep or in trance, natural or induced, *i.e..,* in any case in which the body is reduced to a condition of lethargy. It is in trance that it can best be studied, and here our enquirer will soon find proof that consciousness can work apart from the physical organism, unfettered by the laws that bind it while it works on the physical plane. Clairvoyance and clairaudience are among the most interesting of the phenomena that here lie for investigation.

It is not necessary here to give a large number of cases of clairvoyance, for I am supposing that the enquirer intends to study for himself. But I may mention the case of Jane Rider, observed by Dr. Belden, her medical attendant, a girl who could read and write with her eyes carefully covered with wads of cotton wool, coming down from to the middle of the cheek; of a clairvoyant observed by Schelling who announced the death of a relative at a distance of 150 leagues, and stated that the letter containing the news of the death was on its way; of Madame Lagrandré, who diagnosed the internal state of her mother, giving a description that was proved to be correct by the post-mortem examination; of Emma, Dr. Haddock's somnambule, who constantly diagnosed diseases for him. Speaking generally, the clairvoyant can see and describe events which are taking place at a distance, or under circumstances that render physical sight impossible. *How is this done?* The facts are beyond dispute. They require explanation. We say that consciousness can work through senses other than the physical, senses unfettered by the limitations of space which exist for our bodily senses, and cannot by them be transcended. Those who deny the possibility of such working on what we call the astral plane should at least endeavour to present a hypothesis more reasonable than ours. Facts are stubborn things, and we have here a mass of facts proving the existence of conscious activity on a superphysical plane, of sight without eyes, hearing without ears, obtaining knowledge without physical apparatus. In default of any other explanation, the Theosophical hypothesis holds the field.

There is another class of facts: that of etheric and astral appearances, whether of living or dead persons, wraiths, apparitions, doubles, ghosts, etc., etc. Of course the omniscient person of the end of the nineteenth century will sniff with lofty disdain at the mention of such silly superstitions. But sniffs do not abolish facts, and it is a question of evidence. The weight of evidence is enormously on the side of such appearances, and in all ages of the world human testimony has borne witness to their reality. The enquirer whose demand for proof I have in view may well set to work to gather first hand evidence on this head. Of course if he is afraid of being laughed at he had better leave the matter alone, but if he is robust enough to face the ridicule of the superior person he will be amazed at the evidence which he will collect from persons who have themselves come into contact with astral forms. "Illusions! hallucinations! " the superior person will say. But calling names settles nothing. Illusions to which the vast majority of the human race bears witness are at least worthy of study, if human testimony is to be taken as of any worth. There must be something which gives rise to this unanimity of testimony in all ages of the world, testimony which is found today among civilised people, amid railways and electric lights, as well as among barbarous races.

The testimony of millions of Spiritualists to the reality of etheric and astral forms cannot be left out of consideration. When all cases of fraud and imposture are discounted there remain phenomena that cannot be dismissed as fraudulent, and that can be examined by any persons who care to give time and trouble to the investigation. There is no necessity to employ a professional medium; a few friends well know to each other, can carry on their search together; and it is not too much to say that any half-dozen persons, with a little patience and perseverance, may convince themselves of the existence of forces and of intelligences other than those of the physical plane. There is danger in this research to any emotional, nervous, and easily influenced natures, and it is well not to carry the investigations too far, for the reasons given on the previous pages. But there is no readier way of breaking down the unbelief in the existence of anything outside the physical plane than trying a few experiments, and it is worth while to run some risk in order to effect this breaking down.

These are but hints as to lines that the enquirer may follow, so as to convince himself that there is a state of consciousness such as we label "astral". When he has collected evidence enough to make such a state probable to him, it will be time for him to be put in the way of serious study. For real investigation of the astral plane, the student must develop in himself the necessary senses, and to make his knowledge available while he is in the body, he must learn to transfer his consciousness to the astral plane without losing grip of the physical organism, so that he may impress on the physical brain the knowledge acquired during his astral voyagings. But for this he will need to be not a mere enquirer but a student, and he will require the aid and guidance of a teacher. As to finding that teacher, "when the pupil is ready the teacher is always there".

Further proofs of the existence of the astral plane are, at the present time, most easily found in the study of mesmeric and hypnotic phenomena. And here, ere passing to these, I am bound to put in a word of warning. The use of mesmerism and hypnotism is surrounded by danger. The publicity which attends on all scientific discoveries in the West has scattered broadcast knowledge which places within the reach of the criminally disposed powers of the most terrible character, which may be used for the most damnable purposes. No good man or woman will use these powers, if he finds that he possesses them, save when he utilises them purely for human service, without personal end in view, and when he is very sure that he is not by their means usurping control over the will and the actions of another human being. Unhappily the use of these forces is as open to the bad as to the good, and they may be, and are being, used to most nefarious ends. In view of these new dangers menacing individuals and society, each will do well to strengthen the habits of self-control and of concentration of thought and will, so as to encourage the positive mental attitude as opposed to the negative, and thus to oppose a sustained resistance to all influences coming from without. Our loose habits of thought, our lack of distinct and conscious purpose, lay us open to the attacks of the evil-minded hypnotiser, and that this is a real, not a fancied, danger has been already proved by cases that have brought the victims within grasp of the criminal law. It may be hoped that ere long such hypnotic malpractices may be brought within the criminal code.

While thus in the attitude of caution and of self-defence, we may yet wisely study the experiments made public to the world, in our search for preliminary proofs of the existence of the astral plane. For here Western science is on the very verge of discovering some of those "powers" of which Theosophists have said so much, and we have the right to use in justification of our teachings all the facts with which that science may supply us.

Now, one of the most important classes of these facts is that of thoughts rendered visible as forms. A hypnotised person, after being awakened from trance and being apparently in normal possession of his senses, can be made to see any form conceived by the hypnotiser. No word need be spoken, no touch given; it suffices that the hypnotiser should clearly image to himself some idea, and that idea becomes a visible and tangible object to the person under his control. This experiment may be tried in various ways; while the patient is in trance, "suggestion" may be used; that is, the operator may tell him that a bird is on his knee, and on awaking from the trance he will see the bird and will stroke it; or that he has a lampshade between his hands, and on awaking he will press his hands against it, feeling resistance in the empty air; scores of these experiments may be read in Richet or in Binet and Féré. Similar results may be effected without "suggestion", by pure concentration of the thought; I have seen a patient thus made to remove a ring from a person's finger, without word spoken or touch passing between hypnotiser and hypnotised.

The literature of mesmerism and hypnotism in English, French, and German is now very extensive, and it is open to every one. There may be sought the evidence of this creation of forms by thought and will, forms which, *on the astral plane*, are real and objective.

Mesmerism and hypnotism set the intelligence free on this plane, and it works thereon without the hindrance normally imposed by the physical apparatus; it can see and hear on that plane, and sees thoughts as things. Here, again, for real study, it is necessary to learn how thus to transfer the consciousness while retaining hold of the physical organism; but for preliminary inquiry it suffices to study others whose consciousness is artificially liberated without their own volition. This reality of thought images on a superphysical plane is a fact of the very highest importance, especially in its bearing on reincarnation; but it is enough here to point to it as one of the facts which go to show the *prima facie* probability of the existence of such a plane.

Another class of facts deserving study is that which includes the phenomena of thought-transference, and here we reach the lower levels of the mental, or manasic, plane. The *Transactions of the Psychical Research Society* contain a large number of interesting experiments on this subject, and the possibility of the transference of thought from brain to brain without the use of words, or of any means of ordinary physical communication, is on the verge of general acceptance. And two persons, gifted with patience, may convince themselves of this possibility, if they care to devote to the effort sufficient time and perseverance. Let them agree to give, say, ten minutes daily to their experiment, and fixing on the time, let each shut himself up alone, secure from interruption of any kind. Let one be the thought projector, the other the thought-receiver, and it is safer to alternate these positions, in order to avoid risk of one becoming permanently abnormally passive. Let the thought projector concentrate himself on a definite thought and the will to impress it on his friend; no other idea than the one must enter his mind; his thought must be concentrated on the one thing, "one–pointed" in the graphic language of Patanjali. The thought-receiver, on the other hand, must render his mind a blank, and must merely note the thoughts that drift into it. These he should put down as they appear, his only care being to remain passive, to reject nothing, to encourage nothing. The thought-projector, on his side, should keep a record of the ideas he tries to send, and at the end of six months the two records should be compared. Unless the persons are abnormally deficient in thought and will, some power of communication will by that time have been established between them: and if they are at all psychic they will probably also have developed the power of see in each other in the astral light.

It may be objected that such an experiment would be wearisome and monotonous. Granted. All first hand investigations into natural laws and forces are wearisome and monotonous. That is why nearly every one prefers second-hand to first-hand knowledge; the "sublime patience of the investigator" is one of the rarest gifts. Darwin would perform an apparently trivial experiment hundreds of times to substantiate one small fact . The supersensuous domains certainly do not need for their conquest less patience and less effort than the sensuous. Impatience never yet accomplished anything in the questioning of nature, and the would-be student must, at the very outset, show the tireless perseverance which can perish but cannot relinquish its hold.

Finally, let me advise the inquirer to keep his eyes open for new discoveries, especially in the sciences of electricity, physics, and chemistry. Let him read Professor Lodge's address to the British Association at Cardiff in the autumn of 1891 and Professor Crookes' address to the Society of Electrical Engineers in London the following November. He will there find pregnant hints of the lines along which Western science is preparing to advance, and he will perchance begin to feel that there may be something in H.P. Blavatsky's statement that the Masters of Wisdom are preparing to give proofs that will substantiate the Secret Doctrine.

The Seven Planes and the principles functioning thereon	
7 x	
6 x	
5 Atmâ. Spirit	Spiritual
4 Buddhi. Spiritual Soul	
3 Manas. Human Soul.	Mental
2 Kâma. Astral or Desire-Body	Astral
1 Prâna. Etheric Double. Dense Physical Body	Physical

Another Division according to the Principles

	7 Atmâ	Spiritual
	6 Buddhi	
	5 Higher Manas	
Principles closely interwoven during earth life. Sometimes called high Psychic Plane	4 Lower Manas	Mental
	3 Kâma	Astral
	2 Prâna. Etheric Double	Physical
	1 Dense Physical Body	

Another Division also according the Principles

7	Atmâ	Spiritual
6	Buddhi	
5	Manas	Mental
4	Kâma	Astral
3	Prâna	Physical
2	Etheric Double	
1	Dense Physical Body	

These two latter divisions are matters of convenience in classification. The first diagram gives the planes themselves as they exist in nature.

For the ultimate in deeply healing and transformative, energy shifting binaural beat Chakra CD's and MP3's
www.chakrahealingsounds.com

MAN AND HIS BODIES

CONTENTS

INTRODUCTION... 65

THE PHYSICAL BODY... 67

THE ASTRAL OR DESIRE BODY... 83

THE MIND BODIES... 99

OTHER VEHICLES... 112

THE MAN... 116

INTRODUCTION

So much confusion exists as to consciousness and its vehicles, the man and the garments that he wears, that it seems expedient to place before Theosophical students a plain statement of the facts so far as they are known to us. We have reached a point in our studies at which much that was at first obscure has become clear, much that was vague has become definite, much that was accepted as theory has become matter of first-hand knowledge. It is therefore possible to arrange ascertained facts in a definite sequence, facts which can be observed again and again as successive students develop the power of observation, and to speak on them with the same certainty as is felt by the physicist who deals with other observed and tabulated phenomena. But just as the physicist may err so may the metaphysicist, and as knowledge widens new lights are thrown on old facts, their relations are more clearly seen, and their appearance changes - often because the further light shows that the fact which seemed a whole was only a fragment. No authority is claimed for the views here presented; they are offered only as from a student to students, as an effort to reproduce what has been taught but has doubtless been very imperfectly apprehended, together with such results of the observations of pupils as their limited powers enable them to make.

At the outset of our study it is necessary that the Western reader should change the attitude in which he has been accustomed to regard himself, and that he should clearly distinguish between the man and the bodies in which the man dwells. We are too much in the habit of identifying ourselves with the outer garments that we wear, too apt to think of ourselves as though we were our bodies; and it is necessary, if we are to grasp a true conception of our subject, that we shall leave this point of view and shall cease to identify ourselves with casings that we put on for a time and again cast off, to put on fresh ones when we are again in need of such vestures. To identify ourselves with these bodies that have only a passing existence is really as foolish and as unreasonable as it would be to identify ourselves with our clothes; we are not dependent on them - their value is in proportion to their utility. The blunder so constantly made of identifying the consciousness, which is our Self, with the vehicles in which that consciousness is for the moment functioning, can only be excused by the fact that the waking consciousness, and to some extent the dream consciousness also, do live and work in the body and are not known apart from it to the ordinary man; yet an intellectual understanding of the real conditions may be gained, and we may train ourselves to regard our Self as the owner of his vehicle and after a time this will by experience become for a definite fact, when we learn to separate our Self from his bodies, to step out of the vehicle, and to know that we exist in a far fuller consciousness outside it then within it, and that we are in no sense dependent upon it; when that is once achieved, any further identification of our Self with our bodies is of course impossible, and we can never again make the blunder of supposing we are what we wear. The clear intellectual understanding at least is within the grasp of all of us, and we may train ourselves in the habitual distinguishment between the Self - the man - and his bodies; even to do this is to step out of the illusion in which the majority are wrapped, and changes our whole attitude towards life and towards the world, lifting us into a serener region above "the changes and chances of this mortal life," placing us above the daily petty troubles which loom so largely to embodied consciousness, showing us the true proportion between the ever-changing and the relatively permanent, and making us feel the difference between the drowning man tossed and buffeted by the waves that smother him, and the man whose feet are on a rock while the surges break harmlessly at its base.

By man I mean the living, conscious, thinking Self, the individual; by bodies, the various casings in which this Self is enclosed, each casing enabling the Self to function in some definite region of the universe. As a man might use a carriage on the land, a ship on the water, an aeroplane in the air, to travel from one place to another, and yet in all places remain himself, so does the Self, the real man, remain himself no matter in what body he is functioning; and as carriage, ship and aeroplane vary in materials and arrangement according to the element in which each is destined to move, so does each body vary according to the environment in which it is to act. One is grosser than another, one shorter-lived than another, one has fewer capacities than another; but all have this in common - that relatively to the man they are transient, his instruments, his servants, wearing out and renewed according to their nature, and adapted to his varying needs, his growing powers. We will study them one by one, beginning with the lowest, and then take the man himself, the actor in all the bodies.

THE PHYSICAL BODY

Under the term physical body must be included the two lower principles of man - called in our old terminology the Sthūla Sharīra and Linga Sharīra - since they both function on the physical plane, are composed of physical matter, are formed for the period of one physical life, are cast off by the man at death, and disintegrate together in the physical world when he passes on into the astral.

Another reason for classing these two principles as our physical body or physical vehicle is that so long as we cannot pass out of the physical world - or plane, we are accustomed to call it - we are using one or other or both of these physical vestures; they both belong to the physical plane by their materials, and cannot pass outside it; consciousness working in them is bound within their physical limitations, and is subject to the ordinary laws of space and time. Although partially separable, they are rarely separated during earthly life and such separation is inadvisable and is always a sign of disease or of ill-balanced constitution.

They are distinguishable by the materials of which they are composed into the gross body and the etheric double, the latter being the exact duplicate of the visible body, particle for particle, and the medium through which play all the electrical and vital currents on which the activity of the body depends. This etheric double has hitherto been called the Linga Sharīra, but it seems advisable, for several reasons, to put an end to the use of the name in this relation. "Linga Sharīra" has from time immemorial been used in Hindu books in another sense, and much confusion arises among students of Eastern literature, whether Easterns or Westerns, in consequence of its arbitrary wresting from its recognized meaning; for this reason, if for no other, it would be well to surrender its improper use. Further, it is better to have English names for the subdivisions of the human constitution, and thus remove from our elementary literature the stumbling block to beginners of a Sanskrit terminology. Also, the name etheric double exactly expresses the nature and constitution of the subtler portion of the physical body, and is thus significant and therefore easy to remember, as every name should be; it is "etheric" because made of ether, "double" because an exact duplicate of the gross body - its shadow, as it were.

Now physical matter has seven subdivisions, distinguishable from each other, and each showing a vast variety of combinations within its own limits. The subdivisions are: solid, liquid, gas, ether, the latter having four conditions as distinct from each other as liquids are distinct from solids and gases. These are the seven states of physical matter, and any portion of such matter is capable of passing into any one of these states, although under what we call normal temperature and pressure it will assume one or other of these as its relatively permanent condition, as gold is ordinarily solid, water is ordinarily liquid, chlorine is ordinarily gaseous. The physical body of man is composed of matter in these seven states - the gross body consisting of solids, liquids and gases; and the etheric double of the four subdivisions of ether, known respectively as Ether I, Ether II, Ether III, and Ether IV.

When the higher Theosophical truths are put before people, we find them constantly complaining that they are too much in the clouds, and asking: "Where ought we to begin? If we want to learn for ourselves and prove the truth of the assertions made, how are we to start? What are the first steps that we should take? What, in fact, is the alphabet of this language in which Theosophists discourse so glibly? What ought we to do, we men and women living in the world, in order to understand and verify these matters, instead of merely taking them on trust from others who say they know?" I am going to try to answer that question in the following pages, so that those who are really in earnest may see the earlier practical steps they ought to take - it being always understood that these steps must belong to a life, the moral, intellectual and spiritual parts of which are also under training. Nothing that a man can do to the physical body alone will turn him into a seer or a saint; but it is also true that inasmuch as the body is an instrument that we have to use, certain treatment of the body is necessary in order that we may turn our footsteps in the direction of the Path; while dealing with the body only will never take us to the heights to which we aspire, still to let the body alone will make it impossible for us to scale those heights at all. The bodies in which he has to live and work are the instruments of the man, and the very first thing we have to realize is this: that the body exists for us, not we for the body; the body is ours to use - we do not belong to it to be used by it. The body is an instrument which is to be refined, to be improved, to be trained, to be moulded into such a form and made of such constituents as may best fit it to be the instrument on the physical plane for the highest purposes of the man. Everything which tends in that direction is to be encouraged and cultivated; everything which goes contrary to it is to be avoided. It does not matter what wishes the body may have, what habits it may have contracted in the past, the body is ours, our servant, to be employed as we desire, and the moment it takes the reins into its own hands and claims to guide the man instead of being [8] guided by the man, at that moment the whole purpose of life is subverted, and any kind of progress is rendered utterly impossible. Here is the point from which any person who is in earnest must start. The very nature of the physical body makes it a thing which can be turned fairly easily into a servant or an instrument. It has certain peculiarities which help us in training it and make it comparatively easy to guide and mould, and one of these peculiarities is that when once it has been accustomed to work along particular lines it will very readily continue to follow those lines of its own accord, and will be quite as happy in doing so as it was previously in going along others. If a bad habit has been acquired, the body will make considerable resistance to any change in that habit; but if it be compelled to alter, if the obstacle it places in the way be overcome, and if it be forced to act as the man desires, then after a short time the body will of its own accord repeat the new habit that the man has imposed on it, and will as contentedly pursue the new method as it pursued the old one to which the man found reason to object.

Let us now turn to the consideration of the dense body that we may roughly call the visible part of the physical body, though the gaseous constituents are not visible to the untrained physical eye. This is the most outward garment of the man, his lowest manifestation, his most limited and imperfect expression of himself.

The Dense Body. — We must delay sufficiently long on the constitution of the body to enable us to understand how it is that we can take this body, purify it, and train it; we must glance at a set of activities which are for the most part outside the control of the will, and then at those which are under that control. Both of these work by means of nervous systems, but by nervous systems of different kinds. One carries on all the activities of the body which maintain its ordinary life, by which the lungs contract, by which the heart pulsates, by which the movements of the digestive system are directed. This is composed of the involuntary nerves, commonly called the "sympathetic system." At one time during the long past of physical evolution during which our bodies were built, this system was under the control of the animal possessing it, but gradually it began to work automatically - it passed away from the control of the will, took on its own quasi-independence and carried on all the normal vital activities of the body. While a person is in health, he does not notice these activities; he knows that he breathes when the breathing is oppressed or checked, he knows that his heart beats when the beating is violent or irregular, but when all is in order these processes go on unnoticed. It is, however, possible to bring the sympathetic nervous system under the control of the will by long and painful practice, and a class of Yogi in India - Hatha Yogis they are called - develop this power to an extraordinary degree, with the object of stimulating the lower psychic faculties. It is possible to evolve these (without any regard to spiritual, moral or intellectual growth) by direct action on the physical body. The Hatha Yogi learns to control his breathing even to the point of suspension for a considerable period to control the beating of his heart, quickening or retarding the circulation at will, and by these means to throw the physical body into a trance and set free the astral body. The method is not one to be emulated; but still it is instructive for Western nations (who are apt to regard the body as of such imperative nature) to know how thoroughly a man can bring under his control these normally automatic physical processes, and to realize that thousands of men impose on themselves a long and exquisitely painful discipline in order to see themselves free from the prison-house of the physical body, and to know that they live when the animation of the body is suspended. They are at least in earnest, and are no longer the mere slaves of the senses.

Passing from this we have the voluntary nervous system, one far more important for our mental purposes. This is the great system which is our instrument of thought, by which we feel and move on the physical plane. It consists of the cerebro-spinal axis - the brain and spinal cord - whence go to every part of the body filaments of nervous matter, the sensory and motor nerves - the nerves by which we feel running from the periphery to the axis, and the nerves by which we move running from the axis to the periphery. From every part of the body the nerve-threads run, associating with each other to make bundles, these proceeding to join the spinal cord, forming its external fibrous substance, and passing upwards to spread out and ramify in the brain, the centre of all feeling and all purposive motion controllable by the will. This is the system through which the man expresses his will and his consciousness, and these may be said to be seated in the brain. The man can do nothing on the physical plane except through the brain and nervous system; if these be out of order, he can no longer express himself in orderly fashion. Here is the fact on which materialism has based its contention that thought and brain-action vary together; dealing with the physical plane only, as the materialist is dealing, they do vary together, and it is necessary to bring in forces from another plane, the astral, in order to show that thought is not the result of nervous actions. If the brain be affected by drugs, or by disease, or by injury, the thought of the man to whom the brain belongs can no longer find its due expression on the physical plane. The materialist will also point out that if you have certain diseases, thought will be peculiarly affected There is a rare disease, aphasia, which destroys a particular part of the tissue of the brain, near the ear, and is accompanied by a total loss of memory so far as words are concerned; if you ask a person who is suffering from this disease a question, he cannot answer you; if you ask him his name, he will give you no reply; but if you speak his name he will show recognition of it, if you read him some statement he will signify assent or dissent; he is able to think, but unable to speak. I seems as though the part of the brain that has been eaten away were connected with the physical memory of words, so that with the loss of that the man loses on the physical plane the memory of words and is rendered dumb, while he retains the power of thought and can agree or disagree with any proposition made. The materialistic argument at once breaks down, of course, when the man is set free from his imperfect instrument; he is then able to manifest his powers, though he is again crippled when reduced once more to physical expression. The importance of this as regards our present inquiry lies not in the validity or invalidity of the materialistic position, but in the fact that the man is limited in his expression on the physical plane by the capabilities of his physical instrument, and that this instrument is susceptible to physical agents; if these can injure it they can also improve it - a consideration which we shall find to be of vital importance to us.

These nervous systems, like every part of the body, are built up of cell, small definite bodies, with enclosing wall and contents, visible under the microscope, and modified according to their various functions; these cells in their turn are made up of small molecules, and these again of atoms - the atoms of the chemist, each atom being his ultimate indivisible particle of a chemical element. These chemical atoms combine together in innumerable ways to form the gases, the liquids, and the solids of the dense body. Each chemical atom is to the Theosophist a living thing capable of leading its independent life, and each combination of such atoms into a more complex being is again a living thing; also each cell has a life of its own, and all these chemical atoms and molecules and cells are combined together into an organic whole, a body, to serve as vehicle of a loftier form of consciousness than any which they know in their separated lives. Now, the particles of which these bodies are composed are constantly coming and going, these particles being aggregations of chemical atoms too minute to be visible to the naked eye, though many of them are visible under the microscope. If a little blood be put under the microscope, we see moving in it a number of living bodies, the white and red corpuscles, the white being closely similar in structure and activity to ordinary amoebas; in connection with many diseases microbes are found, bacilli of various kinds, and scientists tell us that we have in our bodies friendly and unfriendly microbes, some that injure and others that pounce upon and devour deleterious intruders and effete matter. Some microbes come to us from without that ravage our bodies with disease, others that promote their health, and so these garments of ours are continually changing their materials, which come and stay for a while, and go away to form parts of other bodies - a continual change and interplay.

Now, the vast majority of mankind know little and care less for these facts, and yet on them hinges the possibility of the purification of the dense body, thus rendering it a fitter vehicle for the indwelling man The ordinary person lets his body build itself up anyhow out of the materials supplied to it, without regard to their nature, caring only that they shall be palatable and agreeable to his desires, and not whether they be suitable or unsuitable to the making of a pure and noble dwelling for the Self, the true man that liveth for ever more. He exercises no supervision over these particle as they come and go, selecting none, rejecting none, but letting everything build itself in as it lists, like a careless mason who should catch up any rubbish as materials for his house, floating wool and hairs, mud, chips, sand, nails, offal, filth of any kind - the veriest jerry-builde is the ordinary man with his body. The purifying of the dense body will then consist in a process of deliberate selection of the particles permitted to compose it; the man will take into it in the way of food the purest constituents he can obtain, rejecting the impure and the gross; he knows that by natural change the particles built into it in the days of his careless living will gradually pass away, at least within seven years - though the process may be considerably hastened - and he resolves to build in no more that are unclean; as he increases the pure constituents he makes in his body an army of defenders, that destroy any foul particles that may fall upon it from without or enter it without his consent; and he guards it further by an active will that it shall be pure, which, acting magnetically, continually drives away from his vicinity all unclean creatures that would fain enter his body, and thus shields it from the inroads to which it is liable, while living in an atmosphere impregnated with uncleanliness of every kind.

When a man thus resolves to purify the body and to make it into an instrument fit for the Self to work with, he takes the first step towards the practice of Yoga - a step which must be taken in this or in some other life before he can seriously ask the question, "How can I learn to verify for myself the truths of Theosophy?" All personal verification of superphysical facts depends on the complete subjection of the physical body to its owner, the man; he has to do the verification, and he cannot do it while he is fast bound within the prison of the body, or while that body is impure. Even should he have brought over from better-disciplined lives partially developed psychic faculties, which show themselves despite present unfavourable circumstances, the use of these will be hampered when he is in the physical body, if that body be impure; it will dull or distort the exercise of the faculties when they play through it, and render their reports untrustworthy.

Let us suppose that a man deliberately chooses that he will have a pure body, and that he either takes advantage of the fact that his body completely changes in seven years, or prefers the shorter and more difficult path of changing it more rapidly - in either case he will begin at once to select the materials from which the new clean body is to be built, and the question of diet will present itself. He will immediately begin to exclude from his food all kinds which will build into his body particles which are impure and polluting. He will strike off all alcohol, and every liquor which contains it, because that brings into his physical body microbes of the most impure kinds, products of decomposition; these are not only offensive in themselves, but they attract towards themselves - and therefore towards any body of which they form part - some of the most objectionable of the physically invisible inhabitants of the next plane. Drunkards who have lost their physical bodies, and can therefore no longer satisfy their longing for intoxicants, hang round places where drink is taken, and round those who take it, endeavouring to push themselves into the bodies of people who are drinking, and thus to share the low pleasure to which they surrender themselves. Women of refinement would shrink from their wines if they could see the loathly creatures who seek to partake in their enjoyment, and the close connection which they thus set up with beings of the most repellent type. Evil elementals also cluster round the thoughts of drunkards clad in elemental essence, while the physical body attracts to itself from the surrounding atmosphere other gross particles given off from drunken and profligate bodies, and these also are built into it, coarsening and degrading it. If we look at people who are constantly engaged with alcohol, in manufacturing or distributing spirits, wines, beers, and other kinds of unclean liquors, we can see physically how their bodies have become gross and coarse. A brewer's man, a publican - to say nothing of persons in all ranks of society who drink to excess - these show fully what everyone who builds into his body any of these particles is doing in part and slowly; the more of these he builds in, the coarser will his body become. And so with other articles of diet, flesh of mammals, birds, reptiles and fish, with that of crustaceous creatures and mollusks which feed on carrion - how should bodies made of such materials be refined, sensitive, delicately balanced and yet perfectly healthy, with the strength and fineness of tempered steel, such as the man needs for all the higher kinds of work? Is it necessary again to add the practical lesson that may be learned by looking at the bodies of those living in such surroundings? See the slaughterman and the butcher, and judge if their bodies look like the fittest instruments for employment on high thoughts and lofty spiritual themes. Yet they are only the highly finished products of the forces that work proportionately in all bodies that feed on the impure viands they supply. True, no amount of attention paid to the physical body by the man will of itself give him spiritual life, but why should he hamper himself with an impure body? Why should he allow his powers, whether great or small, to be limited, thwarted, dwarfed in their attempts to manifest by this needlessly imperfect instrument?

There is, however, one difficulty in our way that we cannot overlook; we may take a good deal of pains with the body and may resolutely refuse to befoul it, but we are living among people who are careless and who for the most part know nothing of these facts in nature. In a town like London, or indeed in any Western town, we cannot walk through streets without being offended at every turn, and the more we refine the body the more delicately acute do the physical senses become, and the more we must suffer in a civilization so coarse and animal as is the present. Walking through the poorer and the business streets, where there are beerhouses at every corner, we can scarcely ever escape the smell of drink, the effluvium from one drinking-place overlapping that from the next - even reputedly respectable streets being thus poisoned; so, too, we have to pass slaughter-houses and butchers' shops. Of course one knows that when civilization is a little more advanced better arrangements will be made, and something will be gained when all these unclean things are gathered in special quarters where those can seek them who want them. But meanwhile particles from these places fall on our bodies, and we breathe them in with the air. But as the normally healthy body gives no soil in which disease-microbes can germinate, so the clean body offers no soil in which these impure particles can grow. Besides, as we have seen, there are armies of living creatures that are always at work keeping our blood pure, and these regiments of true lifeguards will charge down upon any poisonous particle that comes into the city of a pure body and will destroy it and cut it to pieces. For us it is to choose whether we will have in our blood these defenders of life, or whether we will [20] people it with the pirates that plunder and slay the good. The more resolutely we refuse to put into the body anything that is unclean, the more shall we be fortified against attacks from without.

Reference has already been made to the automatism of the body, to the fact that it is a creature of habit, and I said that use could be made of this peculiarity. If the Theosophist says to some aspirant who would fain practise Yoga and win entrance to higher planes being: "You must then begin at once to purify the body, and this must precede the attempt to practise a Yoga worthy of the name; for real Yoga is as dangerous to an impure and undisciplined body as a match to a cask of gunpowder"; if the Theosophist should thus speak, he would very probably be met with the answer that health would suffer if such a course were to be adopted. As a dry matter of fact the body does very much care in the long run what you give it, provided that you give it something that will keep it in health; and it will accommodate itself in a short time to a form of pure and nutritious food that you choose to adopt. Just because it is an automatic creature, it will soon stop asking for things that are steadily withheld from it, and if you disregard its demands for the coarse and ranker kinds of food it will soon get into the habit of disliking them. Just as even a moderately natural palate will shrink with a sickening feeling of disgust from the decaying game and venison if yclept* [* Archaic English, meaning 'called' or 'named'.] "high", so a pure taste will revolt against all coarse foods. Suppose that a man has been feeding his body with various kinds of unclean things, his body will demand them imperiously, and he will be inclined to yield to it; but if he pays no attention to it, and goes his own way and not the way of the body, he will find, perhaps to his surprise, that his body will soon recognize its master and will accommodate itself to his orders; presently it will begin to prefer the things that he gives it, and will set up a liking for clean foods and a distaste for unclean. Habit can be used for help as well as for hindrance, and the body yields when it understands that you are the master and that you do not intend the purpose of your life to be interfered with by the mere instrument that is yours for use. The truth is that it is not the body which is chiefly in fault, but Kama, the desire-nature. The adult body has got into the habit of demanding particular things, but if you notice a child, you will find that the child's body does not spontaneously make demands for the things on which adult bodies feast with coarse pleasure; the child's body, unless it has a very bad physical heredity, shrinks from meat and wine, but its elders force meat on it, and the father and mother give it sips of wine from their glasses at dessert, and bid it "be a little man," till the child by its own imitative faculty and by the compulsion of others is turned into evil ways. Then, of course, impure tastes are made, and perhaps old kamic cravings are awakened which might have been starved out, and the body will gradually form the habit of demanding the things upon which it has been fed. Despite all this in the past, make the change, and as you get rid of the particles that crave these impurities you will feel your body altering its habits and revolting against the very smell of the things that it used to enjoy. The real difficulty in the way of the reformation lies in Kāma, not in the body. You do not want to do it; if you did, you would do it. You say to yourself: "After all, perhaps it does not matter so much; I have no psychic faculties, I am not advanced enough for this to make any difference." You will never become advanced if you do not endeavour to live up to the highest that is within your reach - if you allow the desire-nature to interfere with your progress. You say, "How much I should like to possess astral vision, to travel in the astral body! "but when it comes to the point you prefer a "good" dinner. If the prize for giving up unclean food were a million pounds at the end of a year, how rapidly would difficulties disappear and ways be found for keeping the body alive without meat and wine! But when only the priceless treasures of the higher life are offered, the difficulties are insuperable. If men really desired what they pretend to desire, we should have much more rapid changes around us than we now see. But they make believe, and make believe so effectually that they deceive themselves into the idea that they are in earnest, and they come back life after life to live in the same unprogressive manner for thousands of years; and then in some particular life they wonder why they do not advance, and why somebody else has male such rapid progress in this one life while they make none. The man who is in earnest - not spasmodically but with steady persistence - can make what progress he chooses; while the man who is making believe will run round and round the mill-path for many a life to come.

Here, at any rate, in this purification of the body lies the preparation for all Yoga practice - not the whole preparation most certainly, but an essential part of it. This much must suffice as to the dense body, the lowest vehicle of consciousness.

The Etheric Double. — Modern physical science holds that all bodily changes, whether in the muscles, cells, or nerves, are accompanied by electric action, and the same is probably true even of the chemical changes which are continually going on. Ample evidence of this has been accumulated by careful observations with the most delicate galvanometers. Whenever electric action occurs ether must be present, so that the presence of the current is proof of the presence of the ether, which interpenetrates all, surrounds all; no particle of physical matter is in contact with any other particle, but each swings in a field of ether. The Western scientist asserts as a necessary hypothesis that which the trained pupil in East science asserts as a verifiable observation, for as matter of fact ether is as visible as a chair or a table, only a sight different from the normal physical is need to see it. As has already been said, it exists in four modifications, the finest of these consisting of the ultimate physical atoms - not the so-called chemical atom which is really a complex body - ultimate, because they yield astral matter on disintegration.*
[* See *Occult Chemistry* by Annie Besant and C. W. Leadbeater.]

The etheric double is composed of these four ethers which interpenetrate the solid, liquid and gaseous constituents of the dense body, surrounding every particle with an etheric envelope, and thus presenting a perfect duplicate of the denser form. This etheric double is perfectly visible to the trained sight, and is violet-grey in colour, coarse or fine in its texture as dense body is coarse or fine. The four ethers enter into it, as solids, liquids and gases enter into the composition of the dense body, but they can be in coarser or finer combinations just as can the denser constituents; it is important to notice that the dense body and its etheric double vary together as to their quality, so that as the aspirant deliberately and consciously refines his dense body, the etheric double follows suit without his consciousness and without any additional effort.* [* On looking at a man's lower bodies with astral vision, the etheric double (Linga Sharīra) and the astral body (kâmic body) are seen interpenetrating each other, as both interpenetrate the dense physical, and hence some confusion has arisen in the past and the names Linga Sharīra and astral body have been used interchangeably, while the latter name has also been used for the kâmic or desire-body. This loose terminology has caused much trouble, as the functions of the kâmic body, termed the astral body, have often been understood as the functions of the etheric double, also termed the astral body, and the student, unable to see for himself, has been hopelessly entangled in apparent contradictions. Careful observations on the formation of these two bodies now enable us to say definitely that the etheric double is composed of the physical ethers only, and cannot, if extruded leave the physical plane or go far away from its denser counterpart; further, that it is built after the mould given by the Lords of Karma, and is not brought with him by the Ego, but awaits him with the physical body formed upon it. The astral or kâmic body, the desire-body, on the other hand, is composed of astral matter only, is able to range the astral plane when freed from the physical body, and is the proper vehicle of the Ego on that plane; it is brought with him by the Ego when he comes to re-incarnate. Under these circumstances it is better to call the first the etheric double, and the second the astral body, and so avoid confusion.]

It is by means of the etheric double that the life-force, Prâna, runs along the nerves of the body and thus enables them to act as the carriers of motor force and of sensitiveness to external impacts. The powers of thought, of movement and of feeling are not resident in physical or ether nerve-substance; they are activities of the Ego working in his inner bodies, and the expression of them on the physical plane is rendered possible by the life-breath as it runs along the nerve-threads and round the nerve-cells; for Prâna, the life-breath, is the active energy of the Self, as Shrī Shankaracharya has taught us. The function of the etheric double is to serve as the physical medium for this energy, and hence it is often spoken of in our literature as the "vehicle of Prâna".

It may be useful to note that the etheric double is peculiarly susceptible to the volatile constituents of alcohols.

Phenomena connected with the Physical Body. — When a person "goes to sleep" the Ego slips out of the physical body, and leaves it to slumber and so to recuperate itself for the next day's work. The dense body and its etheric double are thus left to their own devices, and to the play of the influences which they attract to themselves by their constitution and habits. Streams of thought-forms from the astral world of a nature congruous with the thought-forms created or harboured by the Ego in his daily life, pass into and out of the dense and etheric brains, and, mingling with the automatic repetitions of vibrations set up in waking consciousness by the Ego, cause the broken and chaotic dreams with which most people are familiar. These broken images are instructive as showing the working of the physical body when it is left to itself; it can only reproduce fragments of past vibrations without rational order or coherence, fitting them together as they are thrown up, however grotesquely incongruous they may be; it is insensible to absurdity or irrationality, content with a phantasmagoria of kaleidoscopic shapes and colours, without even the regularity given by the kaleidoscope mirrors. Looked at in this way, the dense and etheric brains are readily recognized as instruments of thought, not as creators thereof, for we see how very erratic are their creations, when they are left to themselves.

In sleep the thinking Ego slips out of these two bodies, or rather this one body with its visible and invisible parts, leaving them together; in death it slips out for the last time, but with this difference, that it draws out the etheric double with it, separating it from its dense counterpart and thus rendering impossible any further play of the life-breath in the latter as an organic whole. The Ego quickly shakes off the etheric double, which, as we have seen, cannot pass on to the astral plane, and leaves it to disintegrate with its lifelong partner. It will sometimes appear immediately after death to friends at no great distance from the corpse, but naturally shows very little consciousness, and will not speak or do anything beyond "manifesting" itself. It is comparatively easily seen, being physical, and a slight tension of the nervous system will render vision sufficiently acute to discern it. It is also responsible for many "churchyard ghosts," as it hovers over the grave in which its physical counterpart is lying, and is more readily visible than astral bodies for the reason just given. Thus even "in death they are not divided" by more than a few feet of space.

For the normal man it is only at death that this separation takes place, but some abnormal people of the type called mediumistic are subject to a partial division of the physical body during earth-life, a dangerous and fortunately a comparatively rare abnormality which gives rise to much nervous strain and disturbance. When the etheric double is extruded the double itself is rent in twain; the whole of it could not be separated from the dense body without causing the death of the latter, since the currents of the life-breath need its presence for their circulation. Even its partial withdrawal reduces the dense body to a state of lethargy, and the vital activities are almost suspended; extreme exhaustion follows the re-uniting of the severed parts, and the condition of the medium until the normal union is reestablished is one of considerable physical danger. The greater number of the phenomena that occur in the presence of mediums are not connected with this extrusion of the etheric double, but some who have been distinguished for the remarkable character of the [29] materializations which they have assisted in producing offer this peculiarity to observation. I am informed that Mr. Eglinton exhibited this curious physical dissociation to a rare extent, and that his etheric double might be seen oozing from his left side, while his dense body

81

shriveled perceptibly; and that the same phenomenon has been observed with Mr. Husk, whose dense body became too reduced to fill out his clothes. Mr. Eglinton's body once was so diminished in size that a materialized form carried it out and presented it for the inspection of the sitters - one of the few cases in which both medium and materialized form have been visible together in light sufficient to allow of examination. This shrinkage of the medium seems to imply the removal of some of the denser "ponderable" matter from the body - very possibly part of the liquid constituents - but, so far as I am aware, no observations have been made on this point, and it is therefore impossible to speak with any certainty. What is certain is that this partial extrusion of the etheric double results in much nervous trouble, and that it should not be practised by any sensible person if he finds that he is unfortunate enough to be liable to it.

We have now studied the physical body both in its dense and etheric parts, the vesture which the Ego must wear for his work on the physical plane, the dwelling which may be either his convenient office for physical [30] work, or his prison-house of which death alone holds the key. We can see what we ought to have and what we can gradually make - a body perfectly healthy and strong, and at the same time delicately organized refined and sensitive. Healthy it should be - and in the East health is insisted on as a condition of discipleship - for everything that is unhealthy in the body mars it as an instrument of the Ego, and is apt to distort both the impressions sent inwards and the impulses sent outwards. The activities of the Ego are hindered if his instrument be strained or twisted by ill-health. Healthy then, delicately organized, refined, sensitive, repelling automatically all evil influences, automatically receptive of all good - such a body we should deliberately build choosing among all the things that surround us those that conduce to that end, knowing that the task can be accomplished only gradually, but working on patiently and steadily with that object in view. We shall know when we are beginning to succeed even to a very limited extent, for we shall find opening up in us all kinds of powers of perception that we did not before possess We shall find ourselves becoming more sensitive to sounds and sights, to fuller, softer, richer harmonies, to tenderer, fairer, lovelier hues. Just as the painter trains his eye to see the delicacies of colour to which common eyes are blind; just as the musician trains his ear to hear overtones of notes to which common ears are deaf so may we train our bodies to be receptive to the finer vibrations of life missed by ordinary men. True, many unpleasant sensations will come, for the world we are living in is rendered rough and coarse by the humanity that dwells in it: but, on the other hand, beauties will reveal themselves that will repay us a hundred-fold for the difficulties we face and overcome. And this, not that we may possess such bodies for selfish purposes either of vanity or of enjoyment, but in order that we, the men who own them, may own them for wider usefulness, for added strength to serve. They will be more efficient instruments with which to help the progress of humanity, and so more fit to aid in that task of forwarding human evolution which is the work of our great Masters, and in which it may be our privilege to co-operate.

Although we have been only on the physical plane throughout this part of our subject, we may yet see that the study is not without importance, and that the lowest of the vehicles of consciousness needs our attention and will repay our care. These cities of ours, this land of ours, will be cleaner, fairer, better, when this knowledge has become common knowledge, and when it is accepted not only as intellectually probable, but as a law of daily life.

THE ASTRAL OR DESIRE BODY

We have studied the physical body of man both as to its visible and invisible parts, and we understand that man - the living, conscious entity - in his "waking" consciousness, living in the physical world, can only show so much of his knowledge and manifest so much of his powers as he is able to express through his physical body. According to the perfection or imperfection of its development will be the perfection or imperfection of his expression on the physical plane; it limits him while he functions in the lower world, forming a veritable "ring pass-not" around him. That which cannot pass through it cannot manifest on earth, and hence its importance to the developing man. In the same way when the man is functioning without the physical body in another region of the universe, the astral plane or astral world, he is able to express on that plane just so much of his knowledge and his powers, of himself in short, as his astral body enables him to put forth. It is at once his vehicle and his limitation. The man is more than his bodies; he has in him much that he is unable to manifest either on the physical or on the astral plane; but so much as he is able to express may be taken as the man himself in that particular region of the universe. What he can show of himself down here is limited by the physical body; what he can show of himself in the astral world is limited by the astral body; so we shall find as we rise to higher worlds in our study, that more and more of the man is able to express itself as he himself develops in his evolution, and also gradually brings towards perfection higher and higher vehicles of consciousness.

It may be well to remind the reader, as we are entering on fields comparatively untrodden and to the majority unknown, that no claim is here put forward to infallible knowledge or to perfect power of observation. Errors of observation and of inference may be made on planes above the physical as well as on the physical, and this possibility should always be kept in mind. As knowledge increases and training is prolonged, more and more accuracy will be reached, and such errors will thus gradually be eliminated. But as the writer is only a student, mistakes are likely to be made and to need correction in the future. They may creep in on matters of detail, but will not touch the general principles nor vitiate the main conclusions.

First, let the meaning of the words astral plane or astral world be clearly grasped. The astral world is a definite region of the universe, surrounding and interpenetrating the physical, but imperceptible to our [34] ordinary observation because it is composed of a different order of matter. If the ultimate physical atom be taken and broken up, it vanishes so far as the physical world is concerned; but it is found to be composed of numerous particles of the grossest kind of astral matter – the solid matter of the astral world.* [* The word "astral", starry, is not a very happy one, but it has been used during so many centuries to denote super-physical matter that it would now be difficult to dislodge it. It was probably at first chosen by observers in consequence of the luminous appearance of astral as compared with physical matter. The student is advised to read, on this whole subject, Manual No. V., *The Astral Plane*, by C. W. Leadbeater.] We have found seven sub-states of physical matter -

solid, liquid, gaseous, and four etheric - under which are classified the innumerable combinations which make up the physical world. In the same way we have seven sub-states of astral matter corresponding to the physical, and under these may be classified the innumerable combinations which similarly make up the astral world. All physical atoms have their astral envelopes, the astral matter thus forming what may be called the matrix of the physical, the physical being embedded in the astral. The astral matter serves as a vehicle for Jīva, the One Life animating all, and by means of the astral matter currents of Jīva surround, sustain, nourish every particle of physical matter, the currents of Jīva giving rise not only to what a popularly called vital forces, but also to all electric, magnetic, chemical, and other energies, attraction, cohesion, repulsion and the like, all of which are differentiations of the One Life in which universes swim as fishes in the sea. From the astral world, thus intimately interpenetrating the physical, Jīva passes to the ether of the latter, which then becomes the vehicle of all these forces to the lower sub-states of physical matter, wherein we observe their play. If we imagine the physical world to be struck out of existence without any other change being made, we should still have a perfect replica of it in astral matter; and if we further imagine everyone to be dowered with working astral faculties, men and women would at first be unconscious of any difference in their surroundings; "dead" people who wake up in the lower regions of the astral world often find themselves in such a state and believe themselves to be yet living in the physical world. As most of us have not yet developed astral vision, it is necessary to enforce this relative reality of the astral world as a part of the phenomenal universe, and to see it with the mental eye, if not with the astral. It is as real as - in fact, not being quite so far removed from the One Reality, it is more real than - the physical; its phenomena are open to competent observation like those of the physical plane. Just as down here a blind man cannot see physical objects, and as many things can only be observed with the help of apparatus - the microscope, spectroscope, etc. - so is it with the astral plane. Astrally blind people cannot see astral objects at all, and many things escape ordinary astral vision, or clairvoyance. But at the present stage of evolution many people could develop the astral senses and are developing them to some extent, thus enabling themselves to receive the subtler vibrations of the astral plane. Such persons are indeed liable to make many mistakes, as a child makes mistakes when he begins to use physical senses, but these mistakes are corrected by wider experience, and after a time they can see and hear as accurately on the astral as on the physical plane. It is not desirable to force this development by artificial means, for until some amount of physical strength has been evolved the physical world is about as much as can conveniently be managed, and the intrusion of astral sights, sounds and general phenomena is apt to be disturbing and even alarming. But the time comes when this stage is reached and when the relative reality of the astral part of the invisible world is borne in upon the waking consciousness.

For this it is necessary not only to have an astral body, as we all of us have, but to have it fully organized and in working order, the consciousness being accustomed to act in it, not only to act through it on the physical body. Everyone is constantly working through the astral body, but comparatively few work in it separated from the physical. Without the general action through the astral body there would be no connection between the external world and the mind of man, no connection between impacts made on the physical senses and the perception of them by the mind. The impact becomes a sensation in the astral body, and is then perceived by the mind. The astral body, in which are the centres of sensation, is often spoken of as the astral man, just as we might call the physical body the physical man; but it is of course only a vehicle - a sheath, as the Vedāntin would call it - in which the man himself is functioning, and through which he reaches, and is reached by, the grosser vehicle, the physical body.

As to the constitution of the astral body, it is made up of the seven sub-states of astral matter, and may have coarser or finer materials drawn from each of these. It is easy to picture a man in a well-formed astral body; you can think of him as dropping the physical body and standing up in a subtler, more luminous copy of it, visible in his own likeness to clairvoyant vision, though invisible to ordinary sight. I have said "a well-formed astral body," for an undeveloped person in his astral body presents a very inchoate appearance. Its outline is undefined, its materials are dull and ill-arranged, and if withdrawn from the body it is a mere shapeless, shifting cloud, obviously unfit to act as an independent vehicle; it is, in truth, rather a fragment of astral matter than an organized astral body - a mass of astral protoplasm of an amoeboid type. A well-formed astral body means that a man has reached a fairly high level of intellectual culture or of spiritual growth, so that the appearance of the astral body is significant of the progress made by its owner; by the definiteness of it outline, the luminosity of its materials, and the perfection of its organization, one may judge of the stage of evolution reached by the Ego using it.

As regards the question of its improvement - a question important to us all - it must be remembered that the improvement of the astral body hinges on the one side on the purification of the physical body, and on the other on the purification and development of the mind. The astral body is peculiarly susceptible to impressions from thought, for astral matter responds more rapidly than physical to every impulse from the world of mind. For instance, if we look at the astral world we find it full of continually changing shapes; we find there "thought-forms" - forms composed of elemental essence and animated by a thought - and we also notice vast masses of this elemental essence, from which continually shapes emerge and into which they again disappear; watching carefully, we may see that currents of thought thrill this astral matter, that strong thoughts take a covering of it and persist as entities for a long time, while weak thoughts clothe themselves feebly and waver out again, so that all through the astral world changes are ever going on under thought-impulses. The astral body of man, being made of astral matter, shares this readiness to respond to the impact of thought, and thrills in answer to every thought that strikes it, whether the thoughts come from without, from the minds of other men, or come from within, from the mind of its owner.

Let us study this astral body under these impacts from within and without. We see it permeating the physical body and extending around it in every direction like a coloured cloud. The colours vary with the nature of the man, with his lower, animal passional nature, and the part outside the physical body is called the kâmic aura, as belonging to the Kâma or desire-body, commonly called the astral body of man.* [* This separation of the "aura" from the man, as though it were something different from himself, is misleading, although very natural from the point of view of observation. The "aura" is the cloud round the body, in ordinary parlance; really, the man lives on the various planes in such garments as befit each, and all these garments or bodies interpenetrate each other; the lowest and smallest of these is called "the body", and the mixed substances of the other garments are called the aura when they extend beyond that body. The kâmic aura, then, is merely such part of the kâmic body as extends beyond the physical.] For the astral body is the vehicle of man's kâmic consciousness, the seat of all animal passions and desires, the centre of the senses, as already said, where all sensations arise. It changes its colours continually as it vibrates under thought-impacts; if a man loses his temper, flashes of scarlet appear; if he feels love, rose-red thrills through it. If the man's thoughts are high and noble they demand finer astral matter to answer to them, and we trace this action on the astral body in its loss of the grosser and denser particles from each sub-plane, and its gain of the finer and rarer kinds. The astral body of a man whose thoughts are low and animal, is gross, thick, dense and dark in colour - often so dense that the outline of the physical body is almost lost in it; whereas that of an advanced man is fine, clear, luminous and bright in colour - a really beautiful object. In such a case the lower passions have been dominated, and the selective action of the mind has refined the astral matter. By thinking nobly, then, we purify the astral body, even without having consciously worked towards that end. And be it remembered that this inner working exercises a potent influence on the thoughts that are attracted from without to the astral body; a body which is made by its owner to respond habitually to evil thoughts acts as a magnet to similar thought-forms in its vicinity, whereas a pure astral body acts on such thoughts with a repulsive energy, and attracts to itself thought-forms composed of matter congruous with its own.

As said above, the astral body hinges on one side to the physical, and it is affected by the purity or impurity of the physical body. We have seen that the solids, liquids, gases and ethers of which the physical body is composed may be coarse or refined, gross or delicate Their nature will in turn affect the nature of their corresponding astral envelopes. If, unwisely careless about the physical, we build into our dense bodies solid particles of an impure kind, we attract to ourselves the corresponding impure kind of what we will call the solid astral. As we, on the other hand, build into our dense bodies solid particles of purer type, we attract the correspondingly purer type of solid astral matter. As we carry on the purification of the physical body by feeding it on clean food and drink, by excluding from our diet the polluting kinds of aliment - the blood of animals, alcohol and other things that are foul and degrading - we not only improve our physical vehicle of consciousness, but we also begin to purify the astral vehicle and take from the astral world more delicate and finer materials for its construction. The effect of this is not only important as regards the present earth-life, but it has a distinct bearing also - as we shall see later - on the next post-mortem state, on the stay in the astral world, and also on the kind of body we shall have in the next life upon earth.

Nor is this all: the worse kinds of food attract to the astral body entities of a mischievous kind belonging to the astral world, for we have to do not only with astral matter, but also with what are called the elementals of that region. These are entities of higher and lower types existing on that plane, given birth to by the thoughts of men; and there are also in the astral world depraved men, imprisoned in their astral bodies, known as elementaries. The elementals are attracted towards people whose astral bodies contain matter congenial to their nature, while the elementaries naturally seek those who indulge in vices such as they themselves encouraged while in physical bodies. Any person endowed with astral vision sees, as he walks along our London streets, hordes of loathsome elementals crowding round our butchers' shops; and in beer-houses and gin-palaces elementaries specially gather, feasting on the foul emanations of the liquors, and thrusting themselves, when possible, into the very bodies of the drinkers. These beings are attracted by those who build their bodies out of these materials, and such people have these surroundings as part of their astral life. So it goes on through each stage of the astral plane; as we purify the physical we draw to ourselves correspondingly pure stages of the astral matter.

Now, of course, the possibilities of the astral body largely depend on the nature of the materials we build into it; as by the process of purification we make these bodies finer and finer, they cease to vibrate in answer to the lower impulses, and begin to answer to the higher influences of the astral world. We are thus making an instrument which, though by its very nature sensitive to influences coming to it from without, is gradually losing the power of responding to the lower vibrations, and is taking on the power of answering to the higher - an instrument which is tuned to vibrate only to the higher notes. As we can take a wire to produce a sympathetic vibration, choosing to that end its diameter, its length and its tension, so we can attune our astral bodies to give out sympathetic vibrations when noble harmonies are sounded in the world around us. This is not a mere matter of speculation or of theory; it is a matter of scientific fact. As here we tune the wire on the string, so there we can tune the strings of the astral body; the law of cause and effect holds good there as well as here; we appeal to the law, we take refuge in the law, and on that we rely. All we need is knowledge, and the will to put the knowledge into practice. This knowledge you may take and experiment on first, if you will, as a mere hypothesis, congruous with facts known to you in the lower world; later on, as you purify the astral body, the hypothesis will change into knowledge; it will be a matter of your own first-hand observation, so that you will be able to verify the theories you originally accepted only as working hypothesis.

Our possibilities, then, of mastering the astral world, and of becoming of real service there, depend first of all on this process of purification. There are definite methods of Yoga by which development of the astral senses may be helped forward in a rational and healthy way, but it is not of the least use to try to teach these to anyone who has not been using these simple preparatory means of purification. It is a common experience that people are very anxious to try some new and unusual method of progress, but it is idle to instruct people in Yoga when they will not even practice these preparatory stages in their ordinary life. Suppose one began to teach some very simple form of Yoga to an ordinary unprepared person; he would take it up eagerly and enthusiastically because it was new, because it was strange, because he hoped for very quick results, and before he had been working at it for even a year he would get tired of the regular strain of it in his daily life and disheartened by the absence of immediate effect; unused to persistent effort, steadily maintained day after day, he would break down and give up his practice; the novelty outworn, weariness would soon assert itself. If a person cannot or will not accomplish the simple and comparatively easy duty of purifying the physical and astral bodies by using a temporary self-denial to break the bonds of evil habits in eating and drinking, it is idle for him to hanker after more difficult processes which attract by reason of their novelty and would soon be dropped as an intolerable burden. All talk even of special methods is idle until these ordinary humble means have been practiced for some time; but with the purification new possibilities will begin to show themselves. The pupil will find knowledge gradually flow into him, keener vision will awaken, vibrations will reach him from every side, arousing in him response which could not have been made by him in the days of blindness and obtuseness. Sooner or later, according to the Karma of his past, this experience becomes his, and just as a child mastering the difficulties of the alphabet has the pleasure of the book it can read, so the student will find coming to his knowledge and under his control possibilities of which he had not dreamed in his careless days, new vistas of knowledge opening out before him, a wider universe unfolding on every side.

If, now, for a few moments, we study the astral body as regards its functions in the sleeping and waking states, we shall be able easily and rapidly to appreciate its functions when it becomes a vehicle of consciousness apart from the body. If we study a person when he is awake and when he is asleep, we shall become aware of one very marked change as regards the astral body; when he is awake, the astral activities - the changing colours and so on - all manifest themselves in and immediately around the physical body; but when he is asleep a separation has occurred, and we see the physical body - the dense body and the etheric double - lying by themselves on the bed, while the astral body is floating in the air above them. If the person we are studying is one of mediocre development, the astral body when separated from the physical is the somewhat shapeless mass before described; it cannot go far away from its physical body, it is useless as a vehicle of consciousness and the man within it is in a very vague and dream condition, unaccustomed to act away from his physical vehicle; in fact, he may be said to be almost asleep, failing the medium through which he has been accustomed to work, and he is not able to receive definite impressions from the astral world or express himself clearly through the poorly-organized astral body. The centres of sensation in it may be affected by passing thought-forms, and he may answer in it to stimuli that rouse the lower nature; but the whole effect given to the observer is one of sleepiness and vagueness, the astral body lacking all definite activity and floating idly, inchoate, above the sleeping physical form. If anything should occur tending to lead or drive it away from its physical partner, the latter will awaken and the astral will quickly reenter it. But if a person be observed who is much more developed, say one who is accustomed to function in the astral world and to use the astral body for that purpose, it will be seen that when the physical body goes to sleep and the astral body slips out of it, we have the man himself before us in full consciousness; the astral body is clearly outlined and definitely organized, bearing the likeness of the man, and the man is able to use it as a vehicle - a vehicle far more convenient than the physical. He is wide awake, and is working far more actively, more accurately, with greater power of comprehension, than when he was confined in the denser physical vehicle, and he can move about freely and with immense rapidity at any distance, without causing the least disturbance to the sleeping body on the bed.

If such a person has not yet learned to link together his astral and physical vehicles, if there be a break in consciousness when the astral body slips out as he falls asleep, then, while he himself will be wide awake and fully conscious on the astral plane, he will not be able to impress on the physical brain on his return to his denser vehicle the knowledge of what he has been doing during his absence; under these circumstances his "waking" consciousness - as it is the habit to term the most limited form of our consciousness - will not share the man's experiences in the astral world, not because be does not know them, but because the physical organism is too dense to receive these impressions from him. Sometimes, when the physical body awakes, there is a feeling that something has been experienced of which no memory remains; yet this very feeling shows that there has been some functioning of consciousness in the astral world away from the physical body, though the brain is not sufficiently receptive to have even an evanescent memory of what has occurred. At other times, when the astral body returns to the physical, the man succeeds in making a momentary impression on the etheric double and dense body, and when the latter is awake there is a vivid memory of an experience gained in the astral world; but the memory quickly vanishes and refuses to be recalled, every effort rendering success more impossible, as each effort sets up strong vibrations in the physical brain, and still further overpowers the subtler vibrations of the astral. Or yet again, the man may succeed in impressing new knowledge on the physical brain without being able to convey the memory of where or how that knowledge was gained; in such cases ideas will arise in the waking consciousness as though spontaneously generated, solutions will come of problems before uncomprehended, light will be thrown on questions before obscure. When this occurs, it is an encouraging sign of progress, showing that the astral body is well organized and is functioning actively in the astral world, although the physical body is still but very partially receptive. Sometimes, however, the man succeeds in making the physical brain respond, and then we have what is regarded as a very vivid, reasonable and coherent dream, the kind of dream which most [49] thoughtful people have occasionally enjoyed, in which they feel more alive, not less, than when "awake," and in which they may even receive knowledge which is helpful to them in their physical life. All these are stages of progress marking the evolution and improving organization of the astral body.

But, on the other hand, it is well to understand that persons who are making real and even rapid progress in spirituality may be functioning most actively and usefully in the astral world without impressing on the brain when they return the slightest memory of the work in which they have been engaged, although they may be aware in their lower consciousness of an ever-increasing illumination and widening knowledge of spiritual truth. There is one fact which all students may take as a matter of encouragement, and on which they may rely with confidence, however blank their physical memory may be as regards super-physical experiences: as we learn to work more and more for others, as we endeavour to become more and more useful to the world, as we grow stronger and steadier in our devotion to the Elder Brothers of humanity, and seek ever more earnestly to perform perfectly our little share in Their great work, we are inevitably developing that astral body and that power of functioning in it which render us more efficient servants; whether with or without physical memory, we leave our physical prisons in deep sleep and work along useful lines of activity in the astral world, helping people we should otherwise be unable to reach, aiding and comforting in ways we could not otherwise employ. This evolution is going on with those who are pure in mind, elevated in thought, with their hearts set on the desire to serve. They may be working for many a year in the astral world without bringing back the memory to their lower consciousness, and exercising powers for good to the world far beyond anything of which they suppose themselves to be capable: to them, when Karma permits, shall come the full unbroken consciousness which passes at will between the physical and astral worlds; the bridge shall be made which lets the memory cross from the one to the other without effort, so that the man returning from his activities in the astral world will don again his physical vesture without a moment's loss of consciousness. This is the certainty that lies before all those who choose the life of service. They will one day acquire this unbroken consciousness; and then to them life shall no longer be composed of days of memoried work and nights of oblivion, but it will be a continuous whole, the body put aside to take the rest necessary for it, while the man himself uses the astral body for his work in the astral world; then they will keep the links of thought unbroken, knowing when they leave the physical body, knowing while they are passing out of it, knowing their life away from it, knowing when they return and again put it on: thus they will carry on week after week, year after year, the unbroken, unwearied consciousness which gives the absolute certainty of the existence of the individual Self, of the fact that the body is only a garment that they wear, put on and off at pleasure, and not a necessary instrument of thought and life. They will know that so far from its being necessary to either, life is far more active, thought far more untrammelled without it.

When this stage is reached a man begins to understand the world and his own life in it far better than he did before, begins to realize more of what lies in front of him, more of the possibilities of the higher humanity. Slowly he sees that just as man acquires first physical and then astral consciousness, so there stretch above him other and far higher ranges of consciousness that he may acquire one after the other, becoming active on loftier planes, ranging through wider worlds, exercising vaster powers, and all as the servant of the Holy Ones for the assistance and benefit of humanity. Then physical life begins to assume its true proportion, and nothing that happens in the physical world can affect him as it did ere he knew the fuller, richer life, and nothing that death can do can touch him either in himself or in those he desires to assist. The earth-life takes its true place as the smallest part of human activity, and it can never again be as dark as it used to be, for the light of the higher regions shines down into its obscurest recesses.

Turning from the study of the functions and possibilities of the astral body, let us consider now certain phenomena connected with it. It may show itself to other people apart from the physical body, either during or after earth-life. A person who has complete mastery over the astral body can, of course, leave the physical at any time and go to a friend at a distance. If the person thus visited be clairvoyant, *i.e.*, has developed astral sight, he will see his friend's astral body; if not, such visitor might slightly densify his vehicle by drawing into it from the surrounding atmosphere particles of physical matter, and thus "materialize" sufficiently to make himself visible to physical sight. This is the explanation of many of the appearances of friends at a distance, phenomena which are far more common than most people imagine, owing to the reticence of timid folk who are afraid of being laughed at as superstitious. Fortunately that fear is lessening, and if people would only have the courage and common sense to say what they know to be true, we should soon have a large mass of evidence on the appearances of people whose physical bodies are far away from the places where their astral bodies show themselves. These bodies may, under certain circumstances, be seen by those who do not normally exercise astral vision, without materialization being resorted to. If a person's nervous system be overstrained and the physical body be in weak health, so that the pulses of vitality throb less strongly than usual, the nervous activity so largely dependent on the etheric double may be unduly stimulated, and under these conditions the man may become temporarily clairvoyant. A mother, for instance, who knows her son to be dangerously ill in a foreign land, and who is racked by anxiety about him, may thus become susceptible to astral vibrations, especially in the hours of the night at which vitality is at its lowest; under these conditions, if her son be thinking of her, and his physical body be unconscious, so as to permit him to visit her astrally, she will be likely to see him. More often such a visit is made when the person has just shaken off the physical body at death. These appearances are by no means uncommon, especially where the dying person has a strong wish to reach someone to whom he is closely bound by affection, or where he desires to communicate some particular piece of information, and has passed away without fulfilling his wish.

If we follow the astral body after death, when the etheric double has been shaken off as well as the dense body, we shall observe a change in its appearance. During its connection with the physical body the sub-states of astral matter are intermixed with each other, the denser and the rarer kinds inter-penetrating and intermingling. But after death a rearrangement takes place, and the particles of the different sub-states separate from each other, and, as it were, sort themselves out in the order of their respective densities, the astral body thus assuming a stratified condition, or becoming a series of concentric shells of which the densest is outside. And here we are again met with the importance of purifying the astral body during our life on earth, for we find that it cannot, after death, range the astral world at will; that world has its seven sub-planes, and the man is confined to the sub-plane to which the matter of his external shell belongs; as this outermost covering disintegrates he rises to the next sub-plane, and so on from one to another. A man of very low and animal tendencies would have in his astral body much of the grossest and densest kind of astral matter, and this would hold him down on the lowest level of Kâmaloka; until this shell is disintegrated to a great extent the man must remain imprisoned in that section of the astral world, and suffer the annoyances of that most undesirable locality. When this outermost shell is sufficiently disintegrated to allow escape, the man passes to the next level of the astral world, or perhaps it is more accurate to say that he is able to come into contact with the vibrations of the next sub-plane of astral matter, thus seeming to himself to be in a different region: there he remains till the shell of the sixth sub-plane is worn away and permits his passage to the fifth, his stay on each sub-plane corresponding to the strength of those parts of his nature represented in the astral body by the amount of the matter belonging to that sub-plane. The greater the quantity, then, of the grosser sub-states of matter, the longer the stay on the lower kâmalokic levels, and the more we can get rid of those elements here the briefer will be the delay on the other side of death. Even where the grosser materials are not eliminated completely - a process long and difficult being necessary for their entire eradication - the consciousness may during earth-life be so persistently withdrawn from the lower passions that the matter by which they can find expression will cease to function actively as a vehicle of consciousness - will become atrophied, to borrow a physical analogy. In such case, though the man will be held for a short time on the lower levels, he will sleep peacefully through them, feeling none of the disagreeables accompanying them; his consciousness, having ceased to seek expression through such kinds of matter, will not pass outwards through them to contact objects composed of them in the astral world.

The passage through Kâmaloka of one who has so purified the astral body that he has only retained in it the purest and finest elements of each sub-plane - such as would at once pass into the matter of the sub-plane next above if raised another degree - is swift indeed. There is a point known as the critical point between every pair of sub-states of matter; ice may be raised a point at which the least increment of heat will change it into liquid; water may be raised to a point at which the next increment will change it into vapour. So each sub-state of astral matter may be carried to a point of fineness at which any additional refinement would transform it into the next sub-state. If this has be done for every sub-state of matter in the astral body, it has been purified to the last possible degree of delicacy, then its passage through Kâmaloka will be of inconceivable rapidity, and the man will flash through it untrammeled in his flight to loftier regions.

One other matter remains in connection with the purification of the astral body, both by physical and mental processes, and that is the effect of such purification on the new astral body that will in due course of time be formed for use in the next succeeding incarnation. When the man passes out of Kâmaloka into Devachan, he cannot carry thither with him thought-forms of an evil type; astral matter cannot exist on the devachanic level, and devachanic matter cannot answer to the coarse vibrations of evil passions and desires. Consequently all that the man can carry with him when he finally shakes off the remnants of his astral body will be the latent germs or tendencies which, when they can find nutriment or outlet, manifest as evil desires and passions in the astral world. But these he does take with him, and they lie latent throughout his devachanic life. When he returns for rebirth he brings these back with him and throws them outwards; they draw to themselves from the astral world by a kind of magnetic affinity the appropriate materials for their manifestation, and clothe themselves in astral matter congruous with their own nature, so forming part of the man's astral body for the impending incarnation. Thus we are not only living in an astral body now, but are fashioning the type of the astral body which will be ours in another birth - one reason the more for purifying the present astral body to the utmost, using our present knowledge to ensure our future progress.

For all our lives are linked together, and none of them can be broken away from those that lie behind it or from those that stretch in front. In truth, we have but one life in which what we call lives are really only days. We never begin a new life with a clean sheet on which to write an entirely new story; we do but begin a new chapter which must develop the old plot. We can no more get rid of the karmic liabilities of a preceding life by passing through death, than we can get rid of the pecuniary liabilities incurred on one day by sleeping through a night; if we incur a debt today we are not free of it tomorrow, but the claim is presented until it is discharged. The life of man is continuous, unbroken; the earth lives are linked together, and not isolated. The processes of purification and development are also continuous, and must be carried on through many successive earth-lives. Some time or other each of us must begin the work;

some time or other each will grow weary of the sensations of the lower nature, weary of being in subjection to the animals, weary of the tyranny of the senses. Then the man will no longer consent to submit, he will decide that the bonds of his captivity shall be broken. Why, indeed, should we prolong our bondage, when it is in our own power to break it at any moment? No hand can bind us save our own, and no hand save our own can set us free. We have our right of choice, our freedom of will, and inasmuch as one day we shall all stand together in the higher world, why should we not begin at once to break our bondage, and to claim our divine birthright? The beginning of the shattering of the fetters, of the winning of liberty, is when a man determines that he will make the lower nature the servant of the higher, that here on the plane of physical consciousness he will begin the building of the higher bodies, and will seek to realize those loftier possibilities which are his by right divine, and are only obscured by the animal in which he lives.

THE MIND BODIES

We have already studied at some length the physical and astral bodies of man. We have studied the physical both in its visible and invisible parts, working on the physical plane; we have followed the various lines of its activities, have analysed the nature of its growth, and have dwelt upon its gradual purification . Then we have considered the astral body in a similar fashion, tracing its growth and functions, dealing with the phenomena connected with its manifestation on the astral plane, and also with its purification. Thus we have gained some idea of human activity on two out of seven great planes of our universe. Having done so, we can now pass on to the third great plane, the mind world; when we have learned something of this we shall have under our eyes the physical, the astral, and the mental worlds - our globe and the two spheres surrounding it - as a triple region, wherein man is active during his earthly incarnations and wherein he dwells also during the periods which intervene between the death that closes one earth-life and the birth which opens another. These three concentric spheres are man's school-house and kingdom: in them he works out his development, in them his evolutionary pilgrimage; beyond them he may not consciously pass until the gateway of Initiation has opened before him, for out of these three worlds there is no other way.

This third region, that I have called the mind world, includes, though it is not identical with, that which is familiar to Theosophists under the name of Devachan or Devaloka, the land of the Gods, the happy or blessed land, as some translate it. Devachan bears that name because of its nature and condition, nothing interfering with that world which may cause pain or sorrow; it is a specially guarded state, into which positive evil is not allowed to intrude, the blissful resting-place of man in which he peacefully assimilates the fruits of his physical life.

A preliminary word of explanation regarding the mind world as a whole is necessary in order to avoid confusion. While, like the other regions, it is sub-divided into seven sub-planes, it has the peculiarity that these seven are grouped into two sets - a three and a four. The three upper sub-planes are technically called arûpa, or without body, owing to their extreme subtlety, while the four lower are called rûpa, or with body. Man has two vehicles of consciousness, consequently, in which he functions on this plane, to both of which the term mind body is applicable. The lower of these, the one with which we shall first deal, may, however, be allowed to usurp the exclusive use of the name until a better one be found for it; for the higher one is known as the causal body, for reasons which will become clear further on. Students will be familiar with the distinction between the Higher and Lower Manas; the causal body is that of the Higher Manas, the permanent body of the Ego, or man, lasting from life to life; the mind body is that of the Lower Manas, lasting after death and passing into Devachan, but disintegrating when the life on the rûpa levels of Devachan is over.

(a) The Mind Body. — This vehicle of consciousness belongs to, and is formed of, the matter of the four lower levels of Devachan. While it is especially the vehicle of consciousness for that part of the mental plane, it works upon and through the astral and physical bodies in all the manifestations that we call those of the mind in our ordinary waking consciousness. In the undeveloped man, indeed, it cannot function separately on its own plane as an independent

vehicle of consciousness during his earthly life, and when such a man exercises his mental faculties, they must clothe themselves in astral and physical matter ere he can become conscious of their activity. The mind body is the vehicle of the Ego, the Thinker, for all his reasoning work, but during his early life it is feebly organized and somewhat inchoate and helpless, like the astral body of the undeveloped man.

The matter of which the mind body is composed is of an exceedingly rare and subtle kind. We have already seen that astral matter is much less dense than even the ether of the physical plane, and we have now to enlarge our conception of matter still further, and to extend it to include the idea of a substance invisible to astral sight as well as to physical, far too subtle to be perceived even by the "inner" senses of man. This matter belongs to the fifth plane counting downwards, or the third plane counting upwards, of our universe, and in this matter the Self manifests as mind, as in the next below it (the astral) it manifests as sensation. There is one marked peculiarity about the mind body, as its outer part shows itself in the human aura; it grows, increases in size and in activity, incarnation after incarnation, with the growth and development of the man himself. This peculiarity is one to which so far we are now accustomed. A physical body is built incarnation after incarnation, varying according to nationality and sex, but we think of it as very much the same in size since Atlantean days. In the astral body we found growth in organization as the man progressed. But the mind body literally grows in size with the advancing evolution of the man. If we look at a very undeveloped person, we shall find that the mind body is even difficult to distinguish - that it is so little evolved that some care is necessary to see it at all. Looking [63] then at a more advanced man, one who is not spiritual, but who has developed the faculties of the mind, who has trained and developed the intellect, we shall find that the mind body is acquiring a very definite development, and that it has an organization that can be recognized as a vehicle of activity; it is a clear and definitely outlined object, fine in material and beautiful in colour, continually vibrating with enormous activity, full of life, full of vigour, the expression of the mind in the world of the mind.

As regards its nature, then, made of this subtle matter; as regards its functions, the immediate vehicle in which the Self manifests as intellect; as regards its growth, growing life after life in proportion to the intellectual development, becoming also more and more definitely organized as the attributes and the qualities of the mind become more and more clearly marked. It does not, like the astral body, become a distinct representation of the man in form and feature when it is working in connection with the astral and physical bodies; it is oval - egg-like - in outline, interpenetrating of course the physical and astral bodies, and surrounding them with a radiant atmosphere as it develops - becoming, as I said, larger and larger as the intellectual growth increases. Needless to say, this egg-like form becomes a very beautiful and glorious object as the man develops the higher capacities of the mind: it is not visible to astral sight, but is clearly seen by the higher vision which belongs to the world of mind. Just as an ordinary man living in the physical world sees nothing of astral world - though surrounded by it - until the astral senses are opened, so a man in whom only the physical and astral senses are active will see nothing of the mind world, or of forms composed of its matter, unless mental senses be opened, albeit it surrounds us on every side.

These keener senses, the senses which belong to mind world, differ very much from the senses with which we are familiar here. The very word "senses" in fact, is a misnomer, for we ought rather to say mental "sense." The mind comes into contact with the things of its own world as it were directly oven its whole surface. There are no distinct organs for sight, hearing, touch, taste and smell; all the vibrations which we should here receive through separate sense-organs, in that region give rise to all these characteristics once when they come into touch with the mind. The mind body receives them all at one and the same time and is, as it were, conscious all over of everything, which is able to impress it at all.

It is not easy to convey in words any clear idea of the way this sense receives an aggregate of impressions without confusion, but it may perhaps be best described by saying that if a trained student passes into that region, and there communicates with another student, the mind in speaking speaks at once by colour, sound and form, so that the complete thought is conveyed as a coloured and musical picture instead of only a fragment of it being shown, as is done here by the symbols we call words. Some readers may have heard of ancient books written by great Initiates in colour-language, the language of the Gods; that language is known to many chelâs, and is taken, so far as form and colour are concerned, from the mind-world "speech," in which the vibrations from a single thought give rise to form, to colour, and to sound. It is not that the mind thinks a colour, or thinks a sound, or thinks a form; it thinks a thought, a complex vibration in subtle matter, and that thought expresses itself in all these ways by the vibrations set up. The matter of the mind world is constantly being thrown into vibrations which give birth to these colours, to these sounds, to these forms; and if a man be functioning in the mind body apart from the astral and the physical, he finds himself entirely freed from the limitations of their sense-organs, receptive at every point to every vibration that in the lower world would present itself as separate and different from its fellows.

When, however, a man is thinking in his waking consciousness and is working through his astral and physical bodies, then the thought has its producer in the mind body and passes out, first to the astral and then to the physical; when we think, we are thinking by our mind body - that is, the agent of thought, the consciousness which expresses itself as "I". The "I" is illusory, but it is the only "I" known to the majority of us. When we were dealing with the consciousness the physical body, we found that the man himself was not conscious of all that was going on in the physical body itself, that its activities were partially independent of him, that he was not able to think as the tiny separate cells were thinking, that he did not really share the consciousness of the body as a whole. But when we come to the mind body we come to a region so closely identified with the man that it seems to be himself. "I think," "I know" - can we go behind that? The mind is the Self in the mind body, and it is that which for most of us seems the goal of our search after the Self. But this is only true if we are confined to the waking consciousness. Anyone who has learned that the waking consciousness, like the sensations of the astral body, is only a stage of our journey as we seek the Self, and who has further learned to go beyond it, will be aware that this in its turn is but an instrument of the real man. Most of us, however, as I say, do not separate, cannot separate in thought the man from his mind body, which seems to them to be his highest expression, his highest vehicle, the highest self they can in any way touch or realize. This is the more natural and inevitable in that the individual, the man, at this stage of evolution, is beginning to vivify this body and to bring it into preeminent activity. He has vivified the physical body as a vehicle of consciousness in the past, and is using it in the present as a matter of course. He is vivifying the astral body in the backward members of the race, but in very large numbers this work is at least partially accomplished; in this Fifth Race he is working at the mind body, and the special work on which humanity should now be engaged is the building, the evolution of this body.

We are, then, much concerned to understand how the mind body is built and how it grows. It grows by thought. Our thoughts are the materials we build into this mind body; by the exercise of our mental faculties, by the development of our artistic powers, our higher emotions, we are literally building the mind body day by day, each month and year of our lives. If you are not exercising your mental abilities; if, so far as your thoughts are concerned, you are a receptacle and not a creator; if you are constantly accepting from outside instead of forming from within; if, as you go through life, the thoughts of other people are crowding into your mind; if this be all you know of thought and of thinking, then, life after life, your mind body cannot grow; life after life you come back very much as you went out; life after life you remain as an undeveloped individual. [68] For it is only by the exercise of the mind itself, using its faculties creatively, exercising them, working with them, constantly exerting them - it is only by these means that the mind body can develop, and that the truly human evolution can proceed.

The very moment you begin to realize this you will probably try to change the general attitude of your consciousness in daily life; you will begin to watch its working; and as soon as you do this you will notice that, as just said, a great deal of your thinking is not your thinking at all, but the mere reception of the thoughts of other people; thoughts that come you not know how; thoughts that arrive you do not know whence; thoughts that take themselves off again you not know whither; and you will begin to feel, probably with some distress and disappointments that instead of the mind being highly evolved it is little more than a place through which thoughts are passing. Try yourself, and see how much of the content of your consciousness is your own, and how much of it consists merely of contributions from outside. Stop yourself suddenly now and then during the day, and see what you are thinking about, and on such a sudden checking you will probably either find that you are thinking about nothing - a very common experience - or that you are thinking so vague that a very slight impression is made upon anything you can venture to call your mind. When you have tried this a good many times, and by the very trying have become more self-conscious than you were, then begin to notice the thoughts you find in your mind, and see what difference there is between their condition when they came into the mind and their condition when they go out of it - what you have added to them during their stay with you. In this way your mind will become really active, and will be exercising its creative powers, and if you be wise you will follow some such process as this: first, you will choose the thoughts that you will allow to remain in the mind at all; whenever you find in the mind a thought that is good you will dwell upon it, nourish it, strengthen it, try to put into it more than it had at first; and send it out as a beneficent agent into the astral world; when you find in the mind a thought that is evil you will turn it out with all imaginable promptitude. Presently you will find that as you welcome into your mind all thoughts that are good and useful, and refuse to entertain thoughts which are evil, this result will appear: that more and more good thoughts will flow into your mind from without, and fewer and fewer evil thoughts will flow into it. The effect of making your mind full of good and useful thoughts will be that it will act as a magnet for all the similar thoughts that are around you; as you refuse to give any sort of habourage to evil thoughts, those that approach you will be thrown back by an automatic action of the mind itself. The mind body will take on the characteristic of attracting all thoughts that are good from the surrounding atmosphere, and repelling all thoughts that are evil, and it will work upon the good and make them more active, and so constantly gather a mass of mental material which will form its content, and will grow richer every year. When the time comes when the man shall shake off the astral and physical bodies finally, passing into the mind world, he will carry with him the whole of this gathered-up material; he will take with him the content of consciousness into the region to which it properly belongs, and he will use his devachanic life in working up into faculties and powers the whole of the materials which it has stored.

At the end of the devachanic period the mind body will hand on to the permanent causal body the characteristics thus fashioned, that they may be carried on into the next incarnation. These faculties, as the man returns, will clothe themselves in the matter of the rûpa planes of the mind world, forming the more highly organized and developed mind body for the coming earth-life, and they will show themselves through the astral and physical bodies as the "innate faculties," those with which the child comes into the world. During the present life we are gathering together materials in the way which I have sketched; during the devachan life we work up these materials, changing them from separate efforts of thought into faculty of thought, into mental powers and activities. That is the immense change made during the devachanic life, and inasmuch as it is limited by the use we are making of the earth-life, we shall do well to spare no efforts now. The mind body of the next incarnation depends on the work we are doing in the mind body of the present; here is, then, the immense importance to the evolution of the man of the use which he is now making of his mind bodes; it limits his activities in Devachan, and by limiting those activities it limits the mental qualities with which he will return for his next life upon earth. We cannot isolate one life from another, nor miraculously create something out of nothing. Karma brings the harvest according to our sowing: scanty or plentiful is the crop as the labourer gives seed and tillage.

The automatic action of the mind body, spoken of above, may perhaps be better understood if we consider the nature of the materials on which it draws for its building. The Universal Mind, to which it is allied in its inmost nature, is the storehouse in its material aspect from which it draws these materials. They give rise to every kind of vibration, varying in quality and in power according to the combinations made. The mind body automatically draws to itself from the general storehouse matter that can maintain the combinations already existing in it, for there is a constant changing of particles in the mind body as in the physical, and the place of those which leave is taken by similar particles that come. If the man finds that he has evil tendencies and sets to work to change them, he sets up a new set of vibrations, and the mind body, moulded to respond to the old one resists the new, and there is conflict and suffering. But gradually, as the older particles are thrown out and are replaced by others that answer to the new vibrations - being attracted from outside by their very power to respond to them - the mind body changes its character, changes, in fact, its materials, and its vibrations become antagonistic to the evil and attractive to the good. Hence the extreme difficulty of the first efforts, met and combated by the old form-aspect of the mind; hence the increasing ease of right thinking as the old form changes, and finally, the spontaneity and the pleasure that accompany the new exercise.

Another way of helping the growth of the mind body is the practice of concentration; that is, the fixing of the mind on a point and holding it there firmly, not allowing it to drift or wander. We should train ourselves in thinking steadily and consecutively, not allowing our minds to run suddenly from one thing to another, not to fritter their energies away over a large number or insignificant thoughts. It is a good practice to follow a consecutive line of reasoning, in which one thought grows naturally out of the thought that went before it, thus gradually developing in ourselves the intellectual qualities which make our thoughts sequential and therefore essentially rational; for when the mind thus works, thought following thought in definite and orderly succession, it is strengthening itself as an instrument of the Self for activity in the mind world. This development of the power of thinking with concentration and sequence will show itself in a more clearly outlined and definite mind body, in a rapidly increasing growth, in steadiness and balance, the efforts being well repaid by the progress which results from them.

(b) the Causal Body. — Let us now pass on to the second mind body, known by its own distinctive name of causal body. The name is due to the fact that all the causes reside in this body, which manifest themselves as effects on the lower planes. This body is the "body of Manas," the form-aspect of the individual, of the true man.

It is the receptacle, the storehouse, in which all the man's treasures are stored for eternity, and it grows as the lower nature hands up more and more that is worthy to be built into its structure. The causal body is that into which everything is woven which can endure, and in which are stored the germs of every quality, to be carried over to the next incarnation; thus the lower manifestations depend wholly on the growth and development of this man for "whom the hour never strikes."

The causal body, it is said above, is the form-aspect of the individual. Dealing, as we do here, only with the present human cycle, we may say that until that comes into existence there is no man; there may be the physical and etheric tabernacles prepared for his habitation; passions, emotions and appetites may gradually be gathered to form the kâmic nature in the astral body; but there is not man until the growth through the physical and astral planes has been accomplished, and until the matter of the mind world is beginning to show itself within the evolved lower bodies. When, by the power of the Self preparing its own habitation, the matter of the mind plane begins slowly to evolve, then there is a downpouring from the great ocean of Âtmâ-Buddhi which is ever brooding over the evolution of man - and this, as it were, meets the upward-growing, unfolding mind-stuff, comes into union with it, fertilizes it, and at that point of union the causal body, the individual, is formed. Those who are able to see in those lofty regions say that this form-aspect of the true man is like a delicate film of subtlest matter, just visible, marking where the individual begins his separate life; that delicate, colourless film of subtle matter is the body that lasts through the whole of the human evolution, the thread on which all the lives are strung, the reincarnating Sûtrâtmâ, the "thread-self". It is the receptacle of all which is in accordance with the Law, of every attribute which is noble and harmonious, and therefore enduring. It is that which marks the growth of man, the stage of evolution to which he has attained. Every great and noble thought, every pure and lofty emotion, is carried up and worked into his substance.

Let us take the life of an ordinary man and try to see how much of that life will pass upwards for the building of the causal body, and let us imagine it pictorially as a delicate film; it is to be strengthened, to be made beautiful with colour, made active with life, made radiant and glorious, increasing in size as the man grows and develops. At a low stage of evolution he is not showing much mental quality, but rather he is manifesting much passion, much appetite. He feels sensations and seeks them; they are the things to which he turns. It is as though this inner life of the man puts forth a little of the delicate matter of which it is composed, and round that the mind body gathers; and the mind body puts forth into the astral world, and there comes into contact with the astral body, and becomes connected with it, so that a bridge is formed along which anything capable of passing can pass. The man sends his thoughts downwards by this bridge into the world of sensations, of passions, of animal life, and the thoughts intermingle with all these animal passions and emotions; thus the mind body becomes entangled with the astral body and they adhere to each other and are difficult to separate when the time of death comes. But if the man, during the life which he is spending in these lower regions, has an unselfish thought, a thought of service to someone he loves, and makes some sacrifice in order to do service to his friend, he has then set up something that is able to endure, something that is able to live, something that has in it the nature of the higher world; that can pass upwards to the causal body and be worked into its substance, making it more beautiful, giving it perhaps its first touch of intensity of colour; perhaps all through the man's life there will only be a few of these things that are able to endure, to serve as food for the growth of the real man. So the growth is very slow, for all the rest of his life does not aid it; all his evil tendencies born of ignorance and fed by exercise, have their germs drawn inward and thrown into latency, as the astral body which gave them home and form is dissipated in the astral world; they are drawn inward into the mind body and lie latent there, lacking material for expression in the devachanic world; when the mind body in its turn perishes, they are drawn into the causal body, and there still lie latent, as in suspended animation. They are thrown outwards as the Ego, returning to earth-life reaches the astral world, reappearing there as evil tendencies brought over from the past. Thus the causal body may be spoken of as the storehouse of evil as well as good, being all that remains of the man after the lower vehicles are dissipated, but the good is worked into its texture and aids its growth, while the evil, with the exception noted below, remains as germ.

But the evil which a man works in life, when he puts into its execution his thought, does more injury to the causal body than merely to lie latent in it, as the germ of future sin and sorrow. It is not only that the evil does not help the growth of the true man, but where it is subtle and persistent it drags away, if the expression may be permitted, something of the individual himself. If vice be persistent, if evil be continually followed, the mind body becomes so entangled with the astral that after death it cannot free itself entirely, and some of its very substance is torn away from it, and when the astral dissipates this goes back to the mind stuff of the mind world and is lost to the individual; in this way, if we think again of our image of a film, or bubble, it may be to some extent thinned by vicious living - not only delayed in its progress, but something wrought upon it which makes it more difficult to build into. It is as though the film were in some way affected as to capacity of growth, sterilized or atrophied to some extent. Beyond this, in ordinary cases, the harm wrought to the causal body does not go.

But where the Ego has become strong both in intellect and will without at the same time increasing in unselfishness and love, where it contracts itself round its own separated centre instead of expanding as it grows, building a wall of selfishness around it and using its developing powers for the "I" instead of for the all; in such cases arises the possibility alluded to in so many of the world-scriptures, of more dangerous and ingrained evil, of the Ego setting itself consciously against the Law, of fighting deliberately against evolution. Then the causal body itself, wrought on by vibrations on the mental plane of intellect and will, but both turned to selfish ends, shows the dark hues which result from contraction and loses the dazzling radiance which is its characteristic property. Such harm cannot be worked by a poorly developed Ego nor by ordinary passional or mental faults; to effect injury so far-reaching the Ego must be highly evolved, and must have its energies potent on the mânasic plane. Therefore is it that ambition, pride and the powers of the intellect used for selfish aims are so far more dangerous, so far more deadly in their effects, than the more palpable faults of the lower nature, and the "Pharisee" is often further from the "kingdom of God" than "the publican and the sinner." Along this line is developed the "black magician," the man who conquers passion and desire, develops will and the higher powers of the mind, not to offer them gladly as forces to help forward the evolution of the whole, but in order to grasp all he can for himself as unit, to hold and not to share. These set themselves to maintain separation as against unity, they strive to retard instead of to quicken evolution: therefore they vibrate in discord with the whole instead of in harmony, and are in danger of that rending of the Ego which means the loss of all the fruits of evolution.

All of us who are beginning to understand something of this causal body can make its evolution a definite object in our life; we can strive to think unselfishly and so contribute to its growth and activity. Life after life, century after century, millennium after millennium, this evolution of the individual proceeds, and in aiding its growth by conscious effort we are working in harmony with the divine will, and carrying out the purpose for which we are here. Nothing good that is once woven into the texture of this causal body is ever lost, nothing is dissipated: for this is the man that lives forever.

Thus we see that by the law of evolution everything that is evil, however strong for the time it may seem, has within itself the germ of its own destruction, while everything that is good has in it the seed of immortality; the secret of this lies in the fact that everything evil is inharmonious, that it sets itself against the cosmic law; it is therefore sooner or later broken up by that law, dashed into pieces against it, crushed into dust. Everything that is good, on the other hand, being in harmony with the law, is taken on by it, carried forward; it becomes part of the stream of evolution, of that "not ourselves which makes for righteousness," and therefor it can never perish, can never be destroyed. Here lie not only the hope of man but the certainty of his final triumph; however slow the growth, it is there; however long the way, it has its ending. The individual which is our Self is evolving, and cannot now be utterly destroyed; even though by our folly we may make the growth slower than it need be, none the less everything we contribute to it, however little, lasts in it for ever and is our possession for all the ages that lie in front.

OTHER VEHICLES

We may rise one step further, but in doing so we enter a region so lofty that it is well-nigh beyond our treading, even in imagination. For the causal body itself is not the highest, and the "Spiritual Ego" is not Manas, but Manas united to, merged in, Buddhi. This is the culmination of the human evolution, the end of the revolution on the wheel of births and deaths. Above the plane with which we have been dealing lies a yet higher, sometimes called that of Turīya, the plane of Buddhi.* [* This plane has also been called that of Sushupti.] Here the vehicle of consciousness is the spiritual body, the Ânandamayakosha, or body of bliss and into this Yogïs can pass, and in it taste the eternal bliss of that glorious world, and realize in their own consciousness the underlying unity, which then becomes to them a fact of experience and no longer only an intellectual belief. We may read of a time that comes to the man when he has grown in love, wisdom and power, and when he passes through a great gateway, marking a distinct stage in his evolution. It is the gateway of Initiation, and the man led through it by his Master rises for the first time into the spiritual body, and experiences in it the unity which underlies all the diversity of the physical world and all its separateness, which underlies the separateness of the astral plane and even of the mental region. When these are left behind and the man, clothed in the spiritual body, rises beyond them, he then finds for the first time in his experience that separateness belongs only to the three lower worlds; that he is one with all others, and that, without losing self-consciousness, his consciousness can expand to embrace the consciousness of others, can become verily and indeed one with them. There is the unity after which man is always yearning, the unity he has felt as true and has vainly tried to realize on low planes; there it is realized beyond his loftiest dreaming and all humanity is found to be one with his innermost Self.

Temporary Bodies. — We cannot leave out of our review of man's bodies certain other vehicles that are temporary, and may be called artificial, in their character. When a man begins to pass out of the physical body he may use the astral, but so long as he is functioning in that he is limited to the astral world. It is possible, however, for him to use the mind body - that of the Lower Manas - in order to pass into the mental region, and in this he can also range the astral and physical planes without let or hindrance. The body thus used is often called the Mâyâvi Rûpa, or body of illusion, and it is the mind body re-arranged, so to speak, for separate activity. The man fashions his mind body into the likeness of himself, shapes it into his own image and likeness, and is then in this temporary and artificial body free to traverse the three planes at will and rise superior to the ordinary limitations of man. It is this artificial body that is often spoken of in Theosophical books, in which a person can travel from land to land, passing also into the world of mind, learning there new truths, gathering new experience, and bringing back to the waking consciousness the treasures thus collected. The advantage of using this higher body is that it is not subject to deception and glamour on the astral plane as is the astral body. The untrained astral senses often mislead, and much experience is needed ere their reports can be trusted, but this temporarily formed mind body is not subject to such deceptions; it sees with a true vision, it hears with a true hearing; no astral glamour can overpower, no astral illusion can deceive; therefore this body is preferably used by those trained for such journeyings, made when it is wanted, let go again when the purpose for which it was made is served. Thus it is that the student often learns lessons that otherwise could not reach him, and receives instructions from which he would otherwise be entirely shut off.

Other temporary bodies have been called by the name of Mâyâvi Rûpa, but it seems better to restrict the term to the one just described. A man may appear a distance in a body which is really a thought-form more than a vehicle of consciousness, thought clothed in elemental essence of the astral plane. These bodies are, as a rule, merely vehicles of some particular thought, some special volition, and outside this show no consciousness. They need only be mentioned in passing.

The Human Aura. — We are now in a position to understand what the human aura, in its fullest sense, really is. It is the man himself, manifest at once on the four planes of consciousness, and according to its development is his power of functioning on each; it is the aggregate of his bodies, of his vehicles of consciousness; in a phrase, it is the form-aspect of the man. It is thus that we should regard it, and not as a mere ring or cloud surrounding him. Most glorious of all is the spiritual body, visible in Initiates, through which plays the living âtmic fire; this is the manifestation of man on the buddhic plane. Then comes the causal body, his manifestation in the highest mental world, on the arûpa levels of the plane of mind, where the individual has his home. Next the mind body, belonging to the lower mental planes, and the astral, etheric and dense bodies in succession, each formed of the matter of its own region, and expressing the man as he is in each. When the student looks at the human being he sees all these bodies making up the man, showing themselves separately by virtue of their different grades of matter, and thus marking the stage of development at which the man has arrived. As the higher vision is developed the student sees each of these bodies in its full activity. The physical body is visible as a kind of dense crystallization in the centre of the other bodies, the others permeating it and extending beyond its periphery, the physical being the smallest. The astral comes next, showing the state of the kâmic nature that forms so great a part of the ordinary man, full of his passions, lower appetites and emotions, differing in fineness, in colour, as the man is more or less pure - very dense in the grosser types, finer in the more refined, finest of all if the man be far advanced in his evolution. Then the mind body, poorly developed in the majority but beautiful in many, very various in colouring according to the mental and moral type. Then the causal, scarcely visible in most, visible only if careful scrutiny be brought to bear on the man, so slightly is it developed, so comparatively thin is its colouring, so feeble is its activity. But when we come to look at an advanced soul, it is this and the one above it that at once strike the eye as being emphatically the presentation of the man; radiant in light, most glorious and delicate in colouring, showing hues that no language can describe, because they have no place in earth's spectrum - hues not only most pure and beautiful, but entirely different from the colour known on the lower planes, additional ones which show the growth of the man in those higher regions in the loftier qualities and powers that there exist. If the eye be fortunate enough to be blessed with the sight of one of the Great Ones, He appears as this mighty living form of life and colour, radiant and glorious, showing forth His nature by His very appearance to the view: beautiful beyond description, resplendent beyond imagination. Yet what He is, all shall one day become: that which He is in accomplishment dwells in every son of man a possibility.

There is one point about the aura that I may mention as it is one of practical utility. We can to a great extent protect ourselves against the incursions of thoughts from outside by making a spherical wall round us from the auric substance. The aura responds very readily to the impulse of thought, and if by an effort of the imagination we picture its outer edge as densified into a shell we really make such a protective wall around us. This shell will prevent the incoming of the drifting thoughts that fill the astral atmosphere, and thus will prevent the disturbing influence they exercise over the untrained mind. The drain on our vitality that we sometimes feel, especially when we come into contact with people who unconsciously vampirize their neighbours, may also be guarded against by the formation of a shell, and anyone who is sensitive and who finds himself very exhausted by such a drain will do wisely thus to protect himself. Such is the power of human thought on subtle matter that to think of yourself as within such a shell is to have it formed around you.

Looking at human beings around us on every side we may see them in every stage of development, showing themselves forth by their bodies according to the point in evolution which they have reached, living on plane after plane of the universe, functioning in region after region, as they develop the corresponding vehicles of consciousness. Our aura shows just what we are; we add to it as we grow in the true life; we purify it as we live noble and cleanly lives; we weave into it higher and higher qualities.

Is it possible that any philosophy of life should be more full of hope, more full of strength, more full of joy than this? Looking over the world of men with the physical eye only, we see it degraded, miserable, apparently hopeless, as in truth it is to the eye of flesh. But that same world of men appears to us in quite another aspect when seen by the higher vision. We see indeed the sorrow and the misery, we see indeed the degradation and the shape; but we know that they are transient, that they are temporary, that they belong to the childhood of the race, and that the race will out-grow them. Looking at the lowest and vilest, at the most degraded and most brutal, we can yet see their divine possibilities, we can yet realize what they shall be in the years to come. That is the message of hope brought by Theosophy to the Western world, the message of universal redemption from ignorance, and therefore of universal emancipation from misery - not in dream but in reality, not in hope but in certainty. Everyone who in his own life is showing the growth is, as it were, a fresh realization and enforcement of the message; everywhere the first-fruits are appearing, and the whole world shall one day be ripe for harvest, and shall accomplish the purpose for which the Logos gave it birth.

THE MAN

We have now to turn to the consideration of the man himself, no longer studying the vehicles of consciousness but the action of the consciousness on them, no longer looking at the bodies but at the entity who functions in them. By "the man" I mean that continuing individual who passes from life to life, who comes into bodies and again leaves them, over and over again, who develops slowly in the course of ages, who grows by the gathering and by the assimilation of experience, and who exists on that higher mânasic or mental plane referred to in the last chapter. This man is to be the subject of our study, functioning on the three planes with which we are now familiar - the physical, the astral and the mental.

Man begins his experiences by developing self-consciousness on the physical plane; it is here that appears what we call the "waking consciousness," the consciousness with which we are all familiar, which works through the brain and nervous system, by which we reason in the ordinary way, carrying on all logical processes, by which we remember past events of the current incarnation, and exercise judgment in the affairs of life. All that we recognize as our mental faculties is the outcome of the man's work through the preceding stages of his pilgrimage, and his self-consciousness here becomes more and more vivid, more and more active, more and more alive, we may say, as the individual develops, as the man progresses life after life.

If we study a very undeveloped man, we find his self-conscious mental activity to be poor in quality and limited in quantity. He is working in the physical body through the gross and etheric brains; action is continually going on, so far as the whole nervous system is concerned, visible and invisible, but the action is of a very clumsy kind. There is in it very little discrimination, very little delicacy of mental touch. There is some mental activity, but it is of a very infantile or childish kind. It is occupied with very small things; it is amused by very trivial occurrences; the things that attract its attention are things of a petty character; it is interested in passing objects; it likes to sit at a window and look out at a busy street, watching people and vehicles go by, making remarks on them, overwhelmed with amusement if a well-dressed person tumbles into a puddle or is badly splashed by a passing cab. It has not much in itself to occupy its attention, and therefore it is always rushing outwards in order to feel that it is alive; it is one of the chief characteristics of this low stage of mental evolution that the man working at the physical [91] and etheric bodies, and bringing them into order as vehicles of consciousness, is always seeking violent sensations; he needs to make sure that he is feeling and to learn to distinguish things by receiving from them strong and vivid sensations; it is a quite necessary stage of progress, though an elementary one, and without this he would continually be becoming confused, confused between the processes within his vehicle and without it; he must learn the alphabet of the self and the not-self by distinguishing between the objects causing impacts and the sensations caused by impacts, between the stimulus and the feeling. The lowest types of this stage may be seen gathered at street-corners, lounging idly against a wall and indulging occasionally in a few ejaculatory remarks and in cackling outbursts of empty laughter. Anyone able to look into their brains finds that they are receiving somewhat blurred impressions from passing objects, and that the links between these impressions and others like them are very slight. The impressions are more like a heap of pebbles than a well-arranged mosaic.

In studying the way in which the physical and etheric brains become vehicles of consciousness, we have to run back to the early development of the Ahamkâra, or "I-ness", a stage that may be seen in the lower animals around us. Vibrations caused by the impact of external objects are set up in the brain, transmitted by it to the astral body, and felt by the consciousness as sensations before there is any linking of these sensations to the objects that caused them, this linking being a definite mental action - a perception. When perception begins, the consciousness is using the physical and etheric brains as a vehicle for itself, by means of which it gathers knowledge of the external world. This stage is long past in our humanity, of course, but its fleeting repetition may be seen, when the consciousness takes up a new brain in coming to rebirth; the child begins to "take notice," as the nurses say, that is, to relate a sensation arising in itself to an impression made upon its new sheath, or vehicle, by an external object, and thus to "notice" the object, to perceive it.

After a time the perception of an object is not necessary in order that the picture of the object may be present to the consciousness, and it finds itself able to recall the appearance of an object, when it is not contacted by any sense; such a memoried perception is a idea, a concept, a mental image, and these make up the store which the consciousness gathers from the outside world. On these it begins to work, and the first stage of this activity is the arrangement of the ideas, the preliminary to "reasoning" upon them. Reasoning begins by comparing the ideas with each other, and then by inferring relations between them from the simultaneous or sequential happening of two or more of them, time after time. In this process the consciousness has withdrawn within itself, carrying with it the ideas it has made out of perceptions, and it goes (on) to and [projects on] to them something of its own, as when it infers a sequence, relates one thing to another as cause and effect. It begins to draw conclusions, even to forecast future happenings, when it has established a sequence, so that when the perception regarded as "cause" appears, the perception regarded as "effect" is expected to follow. Again, it notices in comparing its ideas that many of them have one or more elements in common, while their remaining constituents are different, and it proceeds to draw these common characteristics away from the rest and to put them together as the characteristics of a class, and then it groups together the objects that possess these, and when it sees a new object which possesses them, it throws it into that class; in this way it gradually arranges into a cosmos the chaos of perceptions with which it began its mental career, and infers law from the orderly succession of phenomena, and the types it finds in nature. All this is the work of the consciousness in and through the physical brain, but even in this working we trace the presence of that which the brain does not supply. The brain merely receives vibrations; the consciousness working in the astral body changes the vibrations into sensations, and in the mental body changes the sensations into perceptions, and then carries on all the processes which, as just said, transform the chaos into cosmos. And the consciousness thus working is, further, illuminated from above with ides that are not fabricated from materials supplied by the physical world, but are reflected into it directly from the Universal Mind. The great "laws of thought" regulate all thinking, and the very act of thinking reveals their pre-existence, as it is done by them and under them, and is impossible without them.

It is unnecessary almost to remark that all the earlier efforts of consciousness to work in the physical vehicle are subject to much error, both from imperfect perception and from mistaken inferences. Hasty inferences, generalizations from limited experience, vitiate many of the conclusions arrived at, and the rules of logic are formulated in order to discipline the thinking faculty and to enable it to avoid the fallacies into which it constantly falls while untrained. But none the less, the attempt to reason, however imperfectly, from one thing to another is a distinct mark of growth in the man himself, for it shows that he is adding something of his own to the information contributed from outside. This working on the collected materials has an effect on the physical vehicle itself. When the mind links two perceptions together, it also sets up - as it is causing corresponding vibrations in the brain - a link between the sets of vibrations from which the perceptions arose. For as the mind body is thrown into activity, it acts on the astral body, and this again on the etheric and dense bodies, and the nervous matter of the latter vibrates under the impulses sent through; this action shows itself as electrical discharges, and magnetic currents play between molecules and groups of molecules causing intricate inter-relations. These leave what we may call a nervous track, a track along which another current will run more easily than it can run, say, athwart it, and if a group of molecules that were concerned in a vibration should be again made active by the consciousness repeating the idea that was impressed upon them, the disturbance there set up readily runs along the track formed between it and another group by a previous linking, and calls that other group into activity, and it sends up to the mind a vibration which, after the regular transformations, presents itself as an associated idea. Hence the great importance of association, this action of the brain being sometimes exceedingly troublesome, as when some foolish or ludicrous idea has been linked with a serious or a sacred one. The consciousness calls up the sacred idea in order to dwell upon it, and suddenly, quite without its consent, the grinning face of the intruding idea, sent up by the mechanical action of the brain, thrusts itself through the doorway of the sanctuary and defiles it. Wise men pay attention to association, and are careful how they speak of the most sacred things, [96] lest some foolish and ignorant person should make a connecting link between the holy and the silly or the coarse, a link which afterwards would be likely to repel itself in the consciousness. Useful is the precept of the great Jewish Teacher: "Give not that which is holy to the dogs, neither cast ye your pearls before swine."

Another mark of progress appears when a man begins to regulate his conduct by conclusions arrived at within instead of by impulses received from without. He is then acting from his own store of accumulated experiences, remembering past happenings, comparing results obtained by different lines of action in the past, and deciding by these as to the line of action he will adopt in the present. He is beginning to forecast, to foresee, to judge of the future by the past, to reason ahead by remembering what has already occurred, and as a man does this there is a distinct growth of him as man. He may still be confined to functioning in his physical brains, he may still be inactive outside them, but he is becoming a developing consciousness which is beginning to behave as an individual, to choose its own road instead of drifting with circumstances, or being forced along a particular line of action by some pressure from without. The growth of the man shows itself in this definite way, and he develops more and more of what is called character, more and more of will-power.

Strong-willed and weak-willed persons are distinguished by their difference in this respect. The weak-willed man is moved from outside, by outer attractions and repulsions, while the strong-willed man is moved from inside, and continually masters circumstances by bringing to bear upon them appropriate forces, guided by his store of accumulated experiences. This store, which the man has in many lives gathered and accumulated, becomes more and more available as the physical brains become more trained and refined, and therefore more receptive: the store is in the man, but he can only use so much of it as he can impress on the physical consciousness. The man himself has the memory and does the reasoning; the man himself judges, chooses, decides: but he has to do all this through his physical and etheric brains; he must work and act by way of the physical body, of the nervous mechanism, and of the etheric organism therewith connected. As the brain becomes more impressible, as he improves its material and brings it more under his control, he is able to use it for better expression of himself.

How, then, shall we, the living men, try to train our vehicles of consciousness in order that they may serve as better instruments? We are not now studying the physical development of the vehicle, but its training by the consciousness that uses it as an instrument of thought. The man decides that in order to make more useful this [98] vehicle of his, to the improvement of which physically he has already directed his attention, he must train it to answer promptly and consecutively to the impulses he transmits to it; in order that the brain may respond consecutively, he will himself think consecutively, and so sending to the brain sequential impulses he will accustom it to work sequentially by linked groups of molecules, instead of by haphazard and unrelated vibrations. The man initiates, the brain only imitates, and unconnected, careless thinking sets up the habit in the brain of forming unconnected vibratory groups. The training has two stages; the man, determining that he will think consecutively, trains his mental body to link though to thought and not to alight anywhere in a casual way; and then, by thinking thus, he trains the brain which vibrates in answer to his thought. In this way the physical organisms - the nervous and the etheric systems - get into the habit of working in a systematic way, and when their owner wants them, they respond promptly and in an orderly fashion; when he require them they are ready to his hand. Between such a trained vehicle of consciousness and one that is untrained, there is the kind of difference that there is between the tools of a careless workman, who leave them dirty and blunt, unfit for use, and those of the man who makes his tools ready, sharpens them and cleans them, so that when they are wanted they are ready to his hand and he can at once use them for the work demanding his attention. Thus should the physical vehicle be ready always to answer to the call of the mind.

The result of such continued working on the physical body will be by no means exhausted in the improved capacity of the brain. For every impulse sent to the physical body has had to pass through the astral vehicle, and has produced an effect upon it also. For, as we have seen, astral matter is far more responsive to thought-vibrations than is physical, and the effect on the astral body of the course of action we have been considering is proportionally great. Under it the astral body assumes a definite outline, a well-organized condition, such as has already been described. When a man has learned to dominate the brain, when he has learned concentration, when he is able to think as he likes and when he likes, a corresponding development takes place in what - if he be physically conscious of it - he will regard as his dream-life. His dreams will become vivid, well-sustained, rational, even instructive. The man is beginning to function in the second of his vehicles of consciousness, the astral body, is entering the second great region or plane of consciousness, and is acting there in the astral vehicle apart from the physical. Let us for a moment consider the difference between two men both "wide-awake," *i.e.*, functioning in the physical vehicle, one of whom is only using his astral body unconsciously as a bridge between the mind and the brain, and the other of whom is using it consciously as a vehicle. The first sees in the ordinary and very limited way, his astral body not yet being an effective vehicle of consciousness; the second uses the astral vision, and is no longer limited by physical matter; he sees through all physical bodies, he sees behind well as in front, walls and other "opaque" substances are to him transparent as glass; he sees astral forms and colours also, auras, elementals, and so on. If he goes to a concert he sees glorious symphonies of colours as the music swells; to a lecture, he sees the speaker's thoughts in colour and form, and so gains a much more complete representation of his thoughts than is possible to one who hears only the spoken words. For the thoughts that issue in symbols as words go out also as coloured and musical forms, and clothed in astral matter impress themselves on the astral body. Where the consciousness is fully awake in that body, it receives and registers the whole of these additional impressions, and many persons will find, if they closely examine themselves, that they do catch from a speaker a good deal more than the mere words convey, even though they may not have been aware of it at the time when they were listening. Many will find in their memory more than the speaker uttered; sometimes a kind suggestion continuing the thought, as though something rose up round the words and made them mean more than they meant to the ear. This experience shows that the astral vehicle is developing, and as the man pays attention to his thinking and unconsciously uses the astral body, it grows and becomes more and more organized.

The "unconsciousness" of people during sleep is due either to the undevelopment of the astral body, or to the absence of connecting conscious links between it and the physical brain. A man uses his astral body during his waking consciousness, sending mind-currents through the astral to the physical brain; but when the physical brain is not in active use, the brain through which the man is in the habit of receiving impressions from without, he is like David in the armor which he had not proved: he is not so receptive to impressions coming to him only through the astral body, to the independent use of which he is not yet accustomed. Further, he may learn to use it independently on the astral plane, and yet not know that he has been using it when he returns to the physical - another stage in the slow progress of the man - and he thus begins to employ it in its own world, before he can make connection between that world and the world below. Lastly, he makes those connections and then he passes in full consciousness from the use of one vehicle to the use of the other, and is free of the astral world. He has definitely enlarged the area of his waking consciousness to include the astral plane, and while in the physical body his astral senses are entirely at his service, he may be said to be living at one and the same time in the two worlds, there being no break, no gulf between them, and he walks the physical world as a man born blind, whose eyes have been opened.

In the next stage of his evolution, the man begins to work consciously on the third, or mental plane; he has long been working on this plane, sending down from it all the thoughts that take such active form in the astral world and find expression in the physical world through the brain. As he becomes conscious in the mind body, in his mental vehicle, he finds that when he is thinking he is creating forms; he becomes conscious of the creative act, though he has long been exercising the power unconsciously. The reader may remember that in one of the letters quoted in the Occult World, a Master speaks of everyone as making thought-forms but draws the distinction between the ordinary man and the Adept, that the ordinary man produces them unconsciously, while the Adept produces them consciously. (The word Adept is here used in a very wide sense to include Initiates of various grades far below that of a "Master".) At this stage of a man's development his powers of usefulness very largely increase, for when he can consciously create and direct a thought-form – an artificial elemental, as it is often called - he can use it to do work in places to which, at the moment, it may not be convenient for him to travel in his mind body. Thus he can work at a distance as well as at hand, and increase his usefulness; he controls these thought-forms from a distance, watching and guiding them as they work, and making them the agents of his will. As the mind body develops, and the man lives and works in it consciously, he knows all the wider and greater life he lives on the mental plane; while he remains in the physical body and is conscious through that of his physical surroundings, he is yet wide-awake and active in the higher world, and he does not need to put the physical body to sleep in order to enjoy the use of the higher faculties. He habitually employs the mental sense, receiving by it impressions of every kind from the mental plane, so that all the mental workings of others are sensed by him as he senses their bodily movements.

When the man has reached this stage of development - a relatively high one, compared with the average, though low when compared with that to which he aspires - he functions then consciously in his third vehicle, or mind body, traces out all he does in it, and experiences its powers and its limitations. Of necessity, also, he learns to distinguish between this vehicle he uses and himself; then he feels the illusory character of the personal "I", the "I" of the mind body and not of the man, and he consciously identifies himself with the individuality that resides in that higher body, the causal, which dwells on the loftier mental planes, those of the arûpa world. He finds that he, the man, can withdraw himself from the mind body, can leave it behind, and, rising higher, yet remain himself; then he knows the many lives are in verity but one life, and that he, the living man, remains himself through all.

And now as to the links - the links between these different bodies. They exist at first without coming into the consciousness of the man. They are there, otherwise he could not pass from the plane of the mind to that of the body, but he is not conscious of their existence, and they are not actively vivified, they are almost like what are called in the physical body rudimentary organs. Every student of biology knows that rudimentary organs are of two kinds: one kind affords the traces of the stages through which the body has passed in evolution, while the other gives hints of the lines of future growth. These organs exist but they do not function; their activity in the physical body is either of the past or of the future, dead or unborn. The links which I venture by analogy to call rudimentary organs of the second kind, connect the dense and etheric bodies with the astral, the astral with the mind body, the mind body with the causal. They exist, but they have to be brought into activity; that is, they have to be developed, and, like their physical types, they can only be developed by use. The life-current flows through them, the mind-current flows through them, and thus they are kept alive and nourished; but they are only gradually brought into functioning activity as the man fixes his attention on them and brings his will to bear on their development. The action of the will begins to vivify these rudimentary links, and, step by step, very slowly perhaps, they begin to function; the man begins to use them for the passage of his consciousness from vehicle to vehicle.

In the physical body there are nervous centres, little groups of nervous cells, and both impacts from without and impulses from the brain pass through these centres. If one of these is out of order, then at once disturbances arise and physical consciousness is disturbed. There are analogous centres in the astral body, but in the undeveloped man they are rudimentary and do not function. These are links between the physical and the astral bodies, between the astral and the mind bodies, and as evolution proceeds they are vivified by the will, setting free and guiding the "serpent-fire", called Kundalini in Indian books. The preparatory stage for the direct action that liberates Kundalini is the training and purifying of the vehicles, for if this be not thoroughly accomplished, the fire is a destructive instead of a vivifying energy. That is why we have laid so much stress on purification and urge it as a necessary preliminary for all true Yoga.

When a man has rendered himself fit to safely receive assistance in the vivifying of these links, such assistance comes to him as a matter of course from those who are ever seeking opportunity to aid the earnest and the unselfish aspirant. Then, one day, the man finds himself slipping out of the physical body while he is wide-awake, and without any break in consciousness he discovers himself to be free. When this has occurred a few times the passage from vehicle to vehicle becomes familiar and easy. When the astral body leaves the physical in sleep, there is a brief period of unconsciousness, and even when the man is functioning actively on the astral plane he fails to bridge over that unconsciousness on his return. Unconscious as he leaves the body, he will probably be unconscious as he re-enters it; there may be full and vivid consciousness on the astral plane, and yet a complete blank may be all that represents it in the physical brain. But when the man leaves the body in waking consciousness, having developed the links between the vehicles into functional activity, he has bridged the gulf; for him it is a gulf no longer, and his consciousness passes swiftly from one plane to the other, and he knows himself as the same man on both.

The more the physical brain is trained to answer to the vibrations from the mind body, the more is the bridging of the gulf between day and night facilitated. The brain becomes more and more the obedient instrument of the man, carrying on its activities under the impulses from his will, and like a well-broken horse answering to the lightest touch of hand or knee. The astral world lies open to the man who has thus unified the two lower vehicles of consciousness, and it belongs to him with all its possibilities, with all its wider powers, its greater opportunities of doing service and of rendering help. Then comes the joy of carrying aid to sufferers who are unconscious of the agent though they feel the relief, of pouring balm into wounds that then seem to heal of themselves, of lifting burdens that become miraculously light to the aching shoulders on which they pressed so heavily.

More than this is needed to bridge over the gulf between life and life; to carry memory through day and night unbrokenly merely means that the astral body is functioning perfectly, and that the links between it and the physical are in full working order. If a man is to bridge over the gulf between life and life he must do very much more than act in full consciousness in the astral body, and more than act consciously in the mind body; for the mind body is composed of the materials of the lower planes of the mânasic world, and reincarnation does not take place from them. The mind body disintegrates in due course, like the astral and physical vehicles, and cannot carry anything across. The whole question on which memory of past lives turns is this: Can the man, or can he not, function on the higher planes of the mânasic world in his causal body? It is the causal body that passes from life to life: it is in the causal body that everything is stored; it is in the causal body that all experience remains, for into it the consciousness is drawn up, and from its plane is the descent made into rebirth. Let us follow the stages of the life out of the physical world, and see how far the sway of King Death extends. The man draws himself away from the dense part of the physical body; it drops off him, goes to pieces, and is restored to the physical world; nothing remains in which the magnetic link of memory can inhere. He is then in the etheric part of the physical body, but in the course of a few hours he shakes that off, and it is resolved into its elements. No memory, then, connected with the etheric brain will help him to bridge the gulf. He passes on into the astral world, remaining there till he similarly shakes off his astral body, and leaves it behind as he had left the physical; the "astral corpse," in its turn, disintegrates, restores its materials to the astral world, and breaks up all that might serve as basis for the magnetic links necessary for memory. He goes onward in his mind body and dwells in the rûpa levels of Devachan, living there for hundreds of years, working up faculties, enjoying fruit. But from this mind body also he withdraws when the time is ripe, taking from it to carry on into the body that endures the essence of all that he has gathered and assimilated. He leaves the mind body behind him, to disintegrate after the fashion of his denser vehicles, for the matter of it - subtle as it is from our standpoint - is not subtle enough to pass onward to the higher planes of the mânasic world. It has to be shaken off, to be left to go back into the materials of its own region, once more a resolution of the combination into its elements. All the way up the man is shaking off body after body, and only on reaching the arûpa planes of the mânasic world can he be said to have passed beyond the regions over which the disintegrating sceptre of Death has sway. He passes finally out of his dominions, dwelling in the causal body over which Death has no power, and in which he stores up all that he has gathered. Hence its very name of causal body, since all causes that affect future incarnations reside in it. He must then begin to act in full consciousness on the arûpa levels of the mânasic world in his causal body ere he can bring memory across the gulf of death. An undeveloped soul, entering that lofty region, cannot keep consciousness there; he enters it, carrying up all the germs of his qualities; there is a touch, a flash of consciousness embracing past and future, and the dazzled Ego sinks downwards towards rebirth. He carries the germs in this causal body and throws outward on each plane those that belong to it; they gather to themselves matters severally befitting them. Thus on the rûpa levels of the lower mânasic world the mental germs draw round them the matter of those levels to form the new mind body, and the matter thus gathered shows the mental characteristics given to it by the germ within it, as the acorn develops into an oak by gathering into it suitable materials from soil and atmosphere. The acorn cannot develop into a birch or a cedar, but only into an oak, and so the mental germ must develop after its own nature and none other. Thus does Karma work in the building of the vehicles, and the man has the harvest of which he sowed the seed. The germ thrown out from the causal body can only grow after its kind, attracting to itself the grade of matter that belongs to it, arranging that matter in its characteristic form, so that it produces the replica of the quality the man made in the past. As he comes into the astral world, the germs are thrown out that belong to that world, and they draw round themselves suitable astral materials and elemental essences. Thus reappear the appetites, emotions and passions belonging to the desire body, or astral body, of the man, reformed in this fashion on his arrival on the astral plane. If, then, consciousness of past lives is to remain, carried through all these processes and all these worlds it must exist in full activity on that high plane of causes, the plane of the causal body. People do not remember their past lives because they are not yet conscious in the causal body as a vehicle; it has not developed functional activity of its own. It is there, the essence of their lives, their real "I", that from which all proceeds, but it does not yet actively function: it is not yet self-conscious, though unconsciously active, and until it is self-conscious, fully self-conscious, the memory cannot pass from plane to plane and therefore from life to life. As the man advances, flashes of consciousness break forth that illumine fragments of the past, but these flashes need to change to a steady light ere any consecutive memory can arise.

It may be asked: Is it possible to encourage the recurrence of such flashes? Is it possible for people to hasten this gradually growing activity of consciousness on the higher planes? The lower man may labour to this end, if he has patience and courage; he may try to live more and more in the permanent self, to withdraw thought and energy more and more, so far as interest is concerned, from the trivialities and impermanences of ordinary life. I do not mean that a man should become dreamy, abstracted and wandering, a most inefficient member of the home and of society; on the contrary, every claim that the world has on him will be discharged, and discharged the more perfectly because of the greatness of the man who is doing it; he cannot do things as clumsily and imperfectly as the less developed man may do them, for to him duty is duty, and as long as anyone or anything has a claim upon him, the debt must be paid to the uttermost farthing; every duty will be fulfilled as perfectly as he can fulfil it, with his best faculties, his best attention.

But his interest will not be in these things, his thoughts will not be bound to their results; the instant that the duty is performed and he is released his thought will fly back to the permanent life, will rise to the higher level with upward-striving energy, and he will begin to live there and to rate at their true worthlessness the trivialities of the worldly life. As he steadily does this, and seeks to train himself to high and abstract thinking, he will begin to vivify the higher links in consciousness and bring into this lower life the consciousness that is himself.

A man is one and the same man on whatever plane he may be functioning, and his triumph is when he functions on all the five planes in unbroken consciousness. Those whom we call the Masters, the "Men made perfect," function in Their waking consciousness, not only on the three lower planes, but on the fourth plane - that plane of unity spoken of in the *Mândûkyopanishad* as the Turîya, and on that yet above it, the plane of Nirvana. In them evolution is completed, this cycle has been trodden to its close, and what they are, all in time shall be who are climbing slowly upwards. This is the unification of consciousness; the vehicles remain for use, but no longer are able to imprison, and the man uses any one of his bodies according to the work that he has to do.

In this way matter, time and space are conquered, and their barriers cease to exist for the unified man. He has found in climbing upwards that there are less and less barriers in each stage: even on the astral plane, matter is much less of a division than it is down here, separating him from his brothers far less effectually. Traveling in the astral body is so swift that space and time may be said to be practically conquered, for although the man knows he is passing through space it is passed through so rapidly that its power to divide friend from friend is lost. Even that first conquest sets at nought physical distance. When he rose to the mental world he found another power his; he thought of a place: he was there; he thought of a friend: the friend was before him. Even on the third plane consciousness transcends the barriers of matter, space and time, and is present anywhere at will. All things that are seen are seen at once, the moment attention is turned to them; all that is heard is heard at a single impression; space, matter and time, as known in the lower worlds, have disappeared, sequence no longer exists in the "eternal now." As he rises yet higher, barriers within consciousness also fall away, and knows himself to be one with other consciousness other living things; he can think as they think, feel as they feel, know as they know. He can make their limitations his for the moment, in order that he can understand exactly how they are thinking, and yet have his own consciousness. He can use his own great knowledge for the helping of the narrower and more restricted thought, identifying himself with it in order gently to enlarge its bounds. He takes on altogether new functions in nature when he is no longer divided from others, but realizes the Self that is one in all and sends down his energies from the plane of unity. With regard even to the lower animals he is able to feel how the world exists to them, so that he can give exactly the help they need, and can supply the aid after which they are blindly groping. Hence his conquest is not for himself but for all, and he wins wider powers only to place them at the service of all lower in the scale evolution than himself; in this way he becomes self-conscious in all the world; for this he learns to be responsive to every cry of pain, to every throb of joy or sorrow. All is reached, all is gained, and the Master is the man "who has nothing more to learn." By this we mean not that all possible knowledge is at any given moment within His consciousness, but that so far as this stage of evolution is concerned there is nothing that to Him is veiled, nothing of which He does not become fully conscious when He turns His attention to it; within this circle of evolution of everything that lives - and all things live - there is nothing He cannot understand, and therefore nothing that He cannot help.

That is the ultimate triumph of man. All that I have spoken of would be worthless, trivial, were it gained for the narrow self we recognize as self down here; all the steps, my reader, to which I have been trying to win you would not be worth the taking did they set you at last on an isolated pinnacle, apart from all the sinning, suffering selves, instead of leading you to the heart of things, where they and you are one. The consciousness of the Master stretches itself out in any direction in which He sends it, assimilates itself with any point to which He directs it, knows anything which He wills to know; and all this in order that He may help perfectly, that there may be nothing that He cannot feel, nothing that He cannot foster, nothing that He cannot strengthen, nothing that He cannot aid in its evolution; to Him the whole world is one vast evolving whole, and His place in it is that of a helper of evolution; He is able to identify Himself with any step, and at that step to give the aid that is needed. He helps the elementary kingdoms to evolve downwards, and, each in its own way, the evolutions of the minerals, plants, animals and men, and He helps them all as Himself. For the glory of His life is that all is Himself and yet He can aid all, in the very helping realizing as Himself that which He aids.

The mystery how this can be gradually unfolds itself as man develops, and consciousness widens to embrace more and more while yet becoming more vivid, more vital, and without losing knowledge of itself. When the point has become the sphere, the sphere finds itself to be the point; each point contains everything and knows itself one with every other point; the outer is found be only the reflection of the inner; the Reality is the One Life, and the difference an illusion that is overcome.

For the ultimate in energy shifting, transformational and healing, binaural beat Chakra healing CD's and MP3's
www.chakrahealingsounds.com

Subliminal and Self Hypnosis CD's and MP3's
www.subliminalselfhypnosis.com